MILLENNIALS IN THE WORKPLACE

Justin Sachs

Published by Motivational Press, Inc.
1777 Aurora Road
Melbourne, Florida, 32935
www.MotivationalPress.com

Manufactured in the United States of America.

ISBN: 978-1-62865-460-8

Contents

Chapter 1 5

THE US VS. THEM MENTALITY

Chapter 2 20

THE MILLENNIALS TAKE OVER

Chapter 3 40

MULTI-TASKING AND MULTI-MODULE

Chapter 4 64

THE PRODUCT OF OUR ENVIRONMENT

Chapter 5 86

DIGITAL NATIVES

Chapter 6 100

NARCISSISM

Chapter 7 114

MILLENNIALS AND INSTITUTIONS

Chapter 8 135

BUILDING COLLABORATION

Chapter 9 159

MILLENNIALS: YOUR GREATEST OPPORTUNITY OR YOUR
GREATEST THREAT

Chapter 1

THE US VS. THEM MENTALITY

ALL HIPSTERS ARE MILLENNIALS, but not all millennials are hipsters. This could be the key to our management and organizational development issues. Once you accept no rational statement can start with "all millennials," we can measure their importance.

This work takes no interest in flannel, facial hair, or men's hair buns. The focus remains on strategies to optimize the apparent and potential, uniquely and patently valuable contributions shaping this contemporary generation.

It is not our job to justify millennials or their character. Enough has been said, often with contempt, about their vision and values. And, these critics often confuse millennial issues with matters of style and taste.

Those who think "they" are too much with "us" prolong the "us vs. them" damage to organizations. Some conflict between generations will always be with us. But, it may be time to run some intervention here.

THE WHY

Millennials hold the future of work in their hands. Their sheer numbers will control the future. "They" have the advantage of mortality.

"They" are telling us in a million direct and indirect ways just what is going to happen in economics, government, diplomacy, education, and work.

"By 2020, millennials will form 50% of the global workforce."[1] Still, in a global economy, their talent remains in high demand. As older generations move on and out of the workplace, millennials will support them. They will be positioned to demand and design work.

"Hiring millennials and keeping them happy will be critical to a company's future. Millennials bring energy, tech savvy and new ideas to companies that live and die on the threshold of innovation."[2] Heidi Farris, VP of Community Engagement and Marketing at Bloomfire, says, "Ask a millennial to do a task and nine times out of ten, the first question they will ask is, 'Why?' It's a shocking response for some of us who were raised in a world where you don't question authority figures, but the truth of the matter is that it's a good question—one we should ask more often."[3]

And, this central question tells us a lot. "Why?" could be the irksome repetitive query that characterizes the 3-year-old. But, "Why?" is also the genuine driving voice of curiosity and solution focus. It assumes all questions have discoverable answers.

The Pew Research Center reports, 61% of them believe there is something unique about their class. They consider themselves "confident, self-expressive, liberal, upbeat and open to change."[4]

Organizational leaders must ask how important these characteristics can be to their purposes. The most educated generation, the most culturally diverse, the most indebted, the most gender and racially mixed,

1   (Millennials at work: Reshaping the Workplace, 2011)

2   (Kaneshige, 2013)

3   (Kaneshige, 2013)

4   (Millennials: Confident. Connected. Open to Change, 2010)

the most adept at fine motor skill, the most inclined to collaborate, such characteristics are valuable to both new born and aging institutions.

Our interest, then, lies not in how we deal with them or what they need to learn from us. Rather, our interest is more passion than curiosity, a passion to learn as much as we can from their interests, goals, and practices.

This interest foregoes nothing. Their managers and organization superiors have much to teach and rights to demand. But, we would do better to forge commonalities in policy, purpose, and practice. We want to understand desirable, purposeful, and possible synergies, mutualities, and osmosis. And, we must develop strategies to optimize their contribution.

REBUILDING FUNDAMENTAL TRUST

As Pew points out, "They embrace multiple modes of self-expression."[5] But, beyond the tattoos, selfies, and social network blather, you will find a yearning for involvement. Raised by single parents in an age of terrorism and polarization, they wary of trusting classic institutions–church, state, education, and business.

To the extent that you can value their self-disclosure, they want what you want:[6] Being a good parent and homeowner positioned to help others. Perhaps surprisingly, they value living a religious life and respect their elders.

There is no evidence that they are anti-business. In fact, Deloitte's research shows "76 percent now regarding business as a force for positive social impact."[7] They remain convinced that they can exert

---

5   (Millennials: Confident. Connected. Open to Change, 2010)

6   (Millennials: Confident. Connected. Open to Change, 2010)

7   ("Pro-business," but expecting more: The Deloitte Millennial Survey 2017, 2017)

positive social change through their work and organizations and often value the employer on that basis alone.

Millennials understand they cannot do it alone. Their perception of group think and group work reflects their ownership of technology. They understand process and shared work. Everything they know and have achieved comes from exchange and transaction. Everything they know tells them every problem has a fix, a coding solution.

They assume everything is or can be integrated, that economy, environment, geopolitics, and business exist simultaneously and concentrically. So, while local may be better for trendy restaurants, nothing organizational is local anymore.

THEIR TWIST ON RESPECT

We reap what we sow. Before you write off millennials for wanting instant satisfaction or trophies for showing up, you should remember who taught and trained them.

They learned a lot on the soccer field in years when "fair" meant "same." And, video gaming rewarded them with stars, bells, and whistles several times a minute. They ate up the respect. The best parenting also showed them the value of demonstrated self-confidence, speaking up for themselves, looking people in the eye, and asserting their take on things. Scouts, choirs, Sunday school, kindergarten, and other organizations involved in their rearing reorganized to enable and facilitate their voices. Older generations devalued hierarchy and then, faulted them for not respecting authority.

The fact is millennials respect their elders, but they also expect treatment as equals. The generations that manage them seem to have a problem with that. "It boils down to listening seriously to the other person's perspective, avoiding high-handed treatment that underscores the recipient's inferior/dependent position, making decisions based on consensus rather than arbitrary opinions, and believing that the other person has valuable contributions to make."[8]

LIFE AS DIGITAL NATIVES

Millennials have been born into a digital age. They have aged with it. So much a part of it, they have no other context.

All things digital form their reality. The youngest of them even have difficulty explaining things analog. Their worldview is so intricately involved with things digital that it appears to be a virtual reality to their elders.

They have an engineer's mentality. They see things in code and binary sequence. And, as engineers, they avoid metaphor, irony, or subtlety. Their thinking is lateral, horizontal, and logical. And, this supports their confidence in decision making.

The same mindset sometimes ignores the dynamic of human relationships and the organic nature of organization. They are alien in a way, so they are often dismissed as different and disruptive.

But, organizational value lies in that difference and disruption. They are activists in a historical era of seismic shifts so powerful that established structures shake. They continue to ask "why" of the most revered institutions and their outcomes. Still, the owners and stakeholders are slow to answer the question they have never asked.

"The term 'digital native' was coined by Marc Prensky, an education consultant, in 2001. He argued that digital-native children have vastly different learning requirements than what he called 'digital immigrants,' and that digital natives 'think and process information fundamentally differently'."[9]

---

8   (Perna, 2016)

9   (Meyer, 2016)

That does not mean they are hard-wired differently; rather, their cognitive abilities have developed differently than other groups. Digital competence is more synonymous with the culture than the age. That is, young people raised in underdeveloped countries are not digital natives simply because of their age grouping.

Despite the feelings of some concerned adults, the generation's obsession with digital is not a moral issue. They are not losing in grace or decency because they are data or gaming oriented. They are not stunted or malformed in character.

Kate Meyer says, "While we did not find Millennials to be a semi-evolved technology-savvy super-generation (or a group of cyborg-like antisocial screen addicts), we did discover that Millennials' early experiences with digital interfaces shaped their behaviours, at least to some extent."[10]

They do not all understand the workings of a computer and are unlikely to repair one. But, they may know their way around a keyboard and the program interfaces well. A childhood spent on Angry Birds®, Mortal Combat®, and Minecraft® does not ensure analytic abilities as much as they do extraordinary fine motor control and manual dexterity.

Joshua Hebert, writing for Fortune, remarked, "As digital natives, millennials are incredible at finding answers and figuring out how to apply new knowledge. What took prior generations days to learn (for example, digging into the Encyclopaedia Britannica) takes them minutes."[11]

For clarity, we need to differentiate some terminology. Indeed, digital tools provide unprecedented access to volumes of data. But, not all millennials understand that the quantity of data is only one metric. The volume does not equal information. It does not approximate the totality of human experience.

---

10 (Meyer, 2016)

11 (Meyer, 2016)

Viewing a striking 18th-century Peruvian portrait online is not the aesthetic experience of looking at it by candlelight. A video explaining how to drive a golf ball straight and far does not equal the actual mind-muscle experience. Online shopping lacks the personal social experience involved in retail stores.

When measured by volume and speed, sourcing digital knowledge is an extraordinary advantage. But, it can deceive the generation that owns it because data is, not of itself, information. So, while millennials can research, gather, and build databases, locating keywords has no relationship to creative thinking. In a sense, they lack an internal quality control filter which often leaves them believing anything that is digital.

Given resources and autonomy, millennials locate answers to problems. But, they are finding known answers to programmed questions. And, they deserve credit for those speedy calculations and solutions. But, that is different from asking a new question, analysing the known, and connecting the dots in what they find.

The Alleged Narcissism of Millennials

Much has been made of their penchant for selfies! The technology that enables their saving, storage, and transmission through email, Instagram, Facebook, and the like is the only thing new about self-awareness.

The history of art, palaeontology, and culture have portraiture at the center. Humans love to see themselves and others. They pay for and sell portraiture. They find it revealing and telling about individuals, situation, and events. And, they have treasured and collected such images for eons.

Every age has taken selfies with whatever technology it had at hand. So, this desire to self-express does not equal self-absorption. Actually, they believe their generation has the power–and unique dedication–to change the world through collective power. "From school uniforms to team learning to community service, Millennials are gravitating toward group activity."[12]

Contradicting the assumption of their narcissism and self-absorption, "'Family' is a keyword for the Millennials, as 'alienation' was for the 1960's Boomers. Born in a divorce culture and aware of the fragility of the American family, these students tend to embrace measures that promise to strengthen or support it."[13]

A best argument goes this way. The social, economic, and technological context that has informed millennials has also designed them, altered their cellular structure, so to speak. Context has shaped their values and valuation processes.

For instance, as divorce increased, children raised in single parent environments learned to distrust and measure hierarchies differently. They try to balance the subsequent insecurity with their individual ability to handle the insecurity. If they do not regress and internalize fears, their healthiest option is self-awareness and self-confidence.

No longer pressed to marry early, they apparently take longer to mature. In fact, they can prolong their self-development, self-discovery, and self-expression. The development also helps them discover and value empathy for issues larger than themselves. So, the same people accused of being self-interested and selfish find and run charity marathons, work well in collaborative teams, and contribute more than they own.

THE WAR ON INSTITUTIONS

Today's institutions are under attack. The changes needed in church, state, military, education, and business are overdue. And, they will not

12   (Howe, 2000)

13   (Wilson, 2008)

be achieved without trauma. That they need reconstruction is not a generation's fault.

The need for an across-the-board paradigm shift is a function of the institutions' age, their inability to adapt, and their poor performance. We are undergoing a generational seismic occurrence, and some institutions will fall. The Washington Post noticed that the results of a Harvard survey of millennial values paralleled views held across the electorate. Chris Cillizza wrote, "There is a feeling that the safety net is gone. In political terms, the conviction that honest brokers simply don't exist leads people to seek sustenance from those who affirm their points of view... The fact that millennials are so distrustful of institutions doesn't make them unique then. It makes them part of a broader cultural trend with dangerous potential political consequences."[14]

Millennials did not cause this. They have been expressive about their concerns for and interest in rescuing, restoring, and reconstructing institutions that matter to them. They seem to understand that organizations are necessary to humans. Organizations expedite human needs and community services.

Organizations have a way of becoming so large and entrenched they cannot respond. They overtax their communities financially and emotionally. They need and deserve disruption and, sometimes, destruction.

In the last few years, we have seen institutions resist, buckle, and fall before concerns over prolonged wars, the proliferation of terrorists, the increased trade in children and women, the inadequacy and unavailability of healthcare, and more. Globalization has wrought extraordinary achievement and leveled playing fields for many. But, its achievement has brought suffering to many unable to keep pace or martial the necessary resources.

14 (Cilliza, 2015)

In all this, we are expected to honor and exploit ethnic and gender diversity faster and farther than current institutions and traditions seem able to bear. This same pressure to act immediately and decisively stretches our patience and the institutions' wherewithal.

In this climate, Senator Ben Sasse (R-Nebraska), a member of Generation X himself, argues with persuasion that we are caught in a perpetual adolescence. He writes of his concern for our loss of a sense of civics. A conservative with only two years in the Senate and probable presidential ambitions, Sasse speaks well and deliberatively in his criticism of the spoiling of American youth, a generation, therefore, incapable of running a sound future nation.

Sen. Sasse writes, "We need curious, critical, engaged young people who can demonstrate initiative and innovation so the United States can compete with a growing list of economic, military, and technological rivals in the twenty-first century."[15] He begs the question that young Americans have indeed given up self-reliance.

And, he opines without balanced evidence, "Obviously, Washington is a terribly broken and dysfunctional place... but the larger share of what ails us as a nation is well upstream from politics. Culturally, we are a mess."[16] Such comments coming from a voice in the current Senate seem naïve and misdirected. If the swamp needs draining, it need not start with the Millennials.

Their generation's support has split among liberal, progressive, and conservative political candidates evenly enough that they cannot be assigned as a whole to one politic or another. Their energy and passion caught observers by surprise, but it does demonstrate their empathy for necessary change and impatience for getting it done. Anonymous anarchy lurks at the edges of their fervor, but Millennials have not yet been co-opted by that violence.

---

15 (Sasse, 2017)

16 (Sasse, 2017)

Millennials seek to deconstruct institutions with a creative disruption and mindfulness that can reconfigure, reconstitute, and reconfirm. There is something rather noble in that.

DRIVE TO COLLABORATE

Millennials are fluid in their relationships. They grew up in mobile situations, moving their family residence more often and farther than their ancestors. Their sense of neighborhood is larger and less parochial than their parents', and they have travelled more at their age than their elders.

On the other hand, they consider themselves experienced and cosmopolitan even though their experience has been largely virtual. They confuse things aged and artisan with things real and weathered. And, they mistake declaration for opinion.

Boomers led lives of Existential anxiety following decades of war and nuclear threats. Millennials matured amid the debris of Jacques Derrida's Deconstruction where all truths are equally relevant and irrelevant. Their only certainty lies in binary systems.

But, to bring this down to specific experiences, you must only picture a handful of kids sitting around and playing competitive video games. Scores and badges dominate the social interaction. Players share clues and cues to move their avatars to virtual goals. During those moments of play, they were all equals regardless of age and other differentiators. They coached each other because all were invested in the same event.

Their predecessors struggled with Japanese models for teamwork and group accountability. They had difficulty surrendering their legacy of self-reliance. Boomers were supposed to be self-made "men." So, this millennial sense of interplay and improvisation has proven priceless.

Millennials trade and exchange information and techniques to solve problems and reach goals. They have become accustomed to such collaboration throughout their school years and are so comfortable with it that they prefer workplaces where this freedom is supported. Results from the Intelligence Group show "88% prefer a collaborative work-culture rather than a competitive one."[17]

They share in process and expect acknowledgement for that. They have sacrificed individual credit for team recognition. And, this produces good work.

THE DIFFERENCES AMONG US

Millennials bring a lot to the table, a table that does not always understand or appreciate their special character. They tell us in a million different ways how different they are, and we need to put value on that difference because their numbers are very much with us.

Millennials are so present in the workforce they may already be your peers or bosses. They are investors and stakeholders as well as a huge market for sales and development. As digital natives, they are fluent in technology and applications, but they also have a confidence in its potential to change things for the better.

Millennials are logical and binary. They think and work expertly on lateral processes. But, they risk accusations of emotional insensitivity and social awkwardness. Still, they are empathetic enough to resent over-institutionalization. They willingly disrupt process and hierarchy to get the task finished and the badges collected.

Millennials are fresh, creative, and innovative in response to challenges they are convinced have solutions. This limits their roles in theory and speculation, but it grounds business purpose.

---

17 (Ashgar, 2014)

Given their potential contribution–positive or negative, businesses need strategic structures to connect with their wants, needs, and values. In the following chapters, we hope to address those business needs with strategic processes and real world business experiences.

REFERENCES

"Pro-business," but expecting more: The Deloitte Millennial Survey 2017. (2017, May 13). Retrieved from Deloitte: https://www2.deloitte.com/global/en/pages/about-deloitte/articles/millennial-survey-pro-business-but-expecting-more.html

Ashgar, R. (2014, Jan 13). *What Millennials Want In The Workplace (And Why You Should Start Giving It To Them).* Retrieved May 16, 2017, from Forbes: https://www.forbes.com/sites/robasghar/2014/01/13/what-millennials-want-in-the-workplace-and-why-you-should-start-giving-it-to-them/#a95c7014c404

Cilliza, C. (2015, Apr 30). *Millennials don't trust anyone. That's a big deal.* Retrieved May 16, 2017, from The Washington Post: https://www.washingtonpost.com/news/the-fix/wp/2015/04/30/millennials-dont-trust-anyone-what-else-is-new/?utm_term=.a2453525bffc

Hebert, J. (26, Jan 2017). *Why Millennials Deserve More Respect at Work.* Retrieved May 13, 2017, from Fortune: http://fortune.com/2017/01/26/millennials-2/

Howe, N. a. (2000). *Millenials are Rising: The Next Great Generation.* New York: Vintage. Retrieved May 15, 2017, from https://books.google.com/books?hl=en&lr=&id=To_Eu9HCNqIC&oi=fnd&pg=PA3&dq=self-absorption+and+millennials&ots=kbTjYjLSCN&sig=e9H-PBl1jXTK8X8hiicAoiGZuLw#v=onepage&q=self-absorption%20and%20millennials&f=false

Kaneshige, T. (2013, Oct 10). *Why Managers Need to Stop Worrying and Love Millennials.* Retrieved May 13, 2017, from CIO: http://www.cio.com/article/2381827/leadership-management/why-managers-need-to-stop-worrying-and-love-millennials.html

Meyer, K. (2016, Jan 3). *Millennials as Digital Natives: Myths and Realities.* Retrieved May 14, 2017, from Neilsen Norman Group: https://www.nngroup.com/articles/millennials-digital-natives/

(2011). *Millennials at work: Reshaping the Workplace.* PWC.com. Retrieved May 12, 2017, from https://www.pwc.com/m1/en/services/consulting/documents/millennials-at-work.pdf

Millennials: Confident. Connected. Open to Change. (2010, Feb 24). Retrieved May 13, 2017, from Pew Rsearch Center: Millennials: Confident. Connected. Open to Change

Perna, M. (2016, Mar 5). *Millennials & Respect: Why It Matters So Much.* Retrieved May 16, 2017, from Linkedin: https://www.linkedin.com/pulse/millennials-respect-why-matters-so-much-mark-perna

Sasse, B. (2017). *The vanishing American Adult: Our Coming of Age Crisis - and How to Rebuid a Culture of Self-Reliance.* New York: St. Martin;s Press.

Wilson, M. a. (2008, Fall). How Generational Theory Can Improve Teaching: Strategies for Working with the "Millennials". *Curresnts in Teaching and Learnng, 1*(1), 29-44. Retrieved May 15, 2017, from https://pdfs.semanticscholar.org/4aec/f98b4cd5c-7dad19e27f1bd85d5befd3e3121.pdf

Chapter 2

THE MILLENNIALS TAKE OVER

G ENERATION Y, the Boomerang Generation, Generation Me, Trophy Kids. Dates have been somewhat arbitrarily assigned to Millennials. They vary by a few years at start and end depending on the research source. So, at the risk of losing my readers, let me get this out of the way.

If we rely on definitions set out by The Center for Generational Kinetics®, the picture looks like this:[18]

» Gen Z, iGen, or Centennials: Born 1996 and later (age <21)

» Millennials or Gen Y: Born 1977 to 1995 (age 22 to 40)

» Generation X: Born 1965 to 1976 (age 41 to 52)

» Baby Boomers: Born 1946 to 1964 (age 53 to 71)

» Traditionalists or Silent Generation: Born 1945 and before (71+)

Most data rely on 2010 census statistics, so nailing down current and comparative numbers is difficult. Census Reporter[19] puts the United States' median age at 37.8 with some 27% of the population at 20 to 40, and 51% of that is female. Based on the U.S. 2010 Census[20], the number is approximately 37% of the population reporting in 2010. But, you should

---

18 (Generational Breakdown: Info About All of the Generations, n.d.)

19 (United States, n.d.)

20 (Age and Sex Composition: 2010 Census Briefs, 2011)

understand that those reporting as age 40 in 2010 are no longer in our count.

Pew Research[21] data sets the 2015 numbers at 18 to 34. This makes them 20 to 36 at this writing in 2017. Pew puts the 2015 Millennial population at 75.4 million Millennials. And, "With immigration adding more numbers to its group than any other, the Millennial population is projected to peak in 2036 at 81.1 million. Thereafter, the oldest Millennial will be at least 56 years of age and mortality is projected to outweigh net immigration. By 2050 there will be a projected 79.2 million Millennials."[22]

Among these circular and contradictory numbers, let's cut to the chase. The generation is annoyingly and simply not discrete in definition. There are more Millennials than Generation X or Baby Boomers. At work or not, they are very much with us and more likely to live longer than their predecessors. Numerous enough, they carry a heavy hammer, big enough to stop the talk about who is the more respectable, productive, and valuable generation.

THE ANSWERS LIE IN THE DATA

To my statistics-fogged brain, the challenge lies in discerning the information in the numbers, ranges, and standard deviations. The further challenge this book presents is a call to define and implement strategies to deal with the inevitable changes statisticians struggle to forecast.

"The millennial generation is the largest age group to emerge since the baby boom generation, and as this group grows significantly as a proportion of the workforce over the next 20 years, employers will need

21 (Fry, 2016)
22 (Fry, 2016)

to make major adjustments in their engagement models. Motivating, engaging, and retaining people will never cease as managerial priorities, but employers will have to consider carefully what strategies they will use to cultivate and retain valuable millennial employees now and into the future?"[23]

So, our interest lies less in the marketing potential in Millennial numbers than it is in what functional role they play in the workforce. More specifically, we look at ways organization development, talent discovery, and executive leadership must adapt if they want to optimize the power among these large numbers.

The data reveals the increasing presence of women in the workforce, increasing ethnic diversity, and increasing numbers of military veterans, LGBTQ members, and alternatively abled workers. Such factors compound the needs of management to understand, develop, and manage.

WOMEN IN THE WORKPLACE

Women make up 50% of the labor pool and workforce. Gender cannot be an issue when talent determines success in global competition. They have grown up in a world where the employment of women has increased across the generations, industry sectors, and skill sets.

According to Price Waterhouse Cooper, "the global female labour force participation rate has been on the rise."[24]

» 552 million women joined the global workforce between 1980 and 2008.

» 1 billion are expected to join in the next decade.

» Millennial women are more highly educated as they enroll in colleges twice as fast as men.

---

23   (Gilbert, 2011)
24   (Flood, 2015)

» Women enter a workplace that looks different and with a different mindset than women before. Because 49% believe they can rise to the most senior executive level, they prefer employment with organizations promising career paths.

» 86% of female workers are in a relationship with a partner who earns the same (42%) or less (24%).

"Having a more diverse set of employees means you have a more diverse set of skills," says Sara Ellison, an MIT economist, which "could result in an office that functions better."[25] But, she notes gender diversity can also contribute to employee dissatisfaction.

Women, then, afford organizations great potential with complex expectations most organizations have failed to anticipate strategically.

THE TRANSITIONAL GENERATION

In terms of race, "Millennials are a transitional generation."[26] Their U.S. numbers include Caucasians, Blacks, Hispanics/Latinos, and Asians reflecting waves of immigration ongoing since the late 20th-century.

But, the generation is also a bridge to a future generation with increasing numbers of blended races and ethnicities. "About half of newborns in America today are non-white, and the Census Bureau projects that the full U.S. population will be majority non-white sometime around 2043."[27]

The force of population diversification is as much a fact as the redistribution of world populations. The more significant factor is the social, political, and ideological impact of the change. Increased diversity will design its future of necessity and accident. But, if organizations

---

25   (Dizikes, 2014)

26   (Millennials in Adulthood: Detached from Institutions, Networked with Friends, 2014)

27   (Millennials in Adulthood: Detached from Institutions, Networked with Friends, 2014)

want to optimize the power within, they must prepare to manage the energies, not the differences, that diverse people bring to the table.

Organizations need understanding, process, and structure. They must invite voices, integrate their input, and share their achievements. And, they must do this in ways defined by those employees as relevant to them.

Where corporations optimize their employees' diversity, McKinsey & Company reports:[28]

» Companies in the top quartile for racial and ethnic diversity are 35% more likely to show financial returns above their respective national industry medians.

» Companies in the top quartile for gender diversity are 15% more likely to show financial returns above their respective national industry medians.

» Companies in the bottom quartile both for gender and for ethnicity and race are statistically less likely to achieve above-average financial returns than the average companies in the data set.

» In the United States, there is a linear relationship between racial and ethnic diversity and better financial performance: for every 10% increase in racial and ethnic diversity on the senior-executive team, earnings before interest and taxes (EBIT) rise 0.8 percent.

» Racial and ethnic diversity has a stronger impact on financial performance in the United States than gender diversity, perhaps because earlier efforts to increase women's representation in the top levels of business have already yielded positive results.

» While certain industries perform better on gender diversity and other industries on ethnic and racial diversity, no industry or company is in the top quartile on both dimensions.

---

28 (Hunt, 2015)

» The unequal performance of companies in the same industry and the same country implies that diversity is a competitive differentiator shifting market share toward more diverse companies.

Despite such evidence, LinkedIn, Google, Intel, and more prominent business superstars have been slow to diversify their workforce or organizational leadership. "So, why do companies have so many problems when it comes to recruiting, supporting and promoting people of color in the workplace in a genuine way?"[29] Still, Fortune lists notable leaders in diversity at Teas Healthcare, Delta, Kimpton Hotels, Marriott International, Wegmans Food Markets, Comcast, USAA, Old Navy, and more performance leaders.[30]

Global competition will not wait for organizations to let diversity find its way. If talent makes a difference, they must take aggressive and assertive steps to locate, cultivate, engage, and retain that talent.

OUR VETERANS

The economy has not served military veterans well. It fails to respect their individual talent, personal discipline, and often top-notch training. Millennials have voluntarily served in combat and non-combat roles since before September 11, 2001. And, the numbers would suggest they are finding employment.

"Just over one-third of veterans (7.3 million) served during Gulf War era I (August 1990 to August 2001) or Gulf War era II (September 2001 forward). Another quarter (5.2 million) served outside the designated wartime periods."[31] According to a BLS News Release:

---

29   (Williams)

30   (50 Best Workplaces for Diversity, 2016)

31   (Employment Situation of Veterans — 2016, 2017)

» Unemployment rate for male veterans overall is not statistically different from the rate for female veterans.

» Unemployment rate for male veterans (4.2%) edged down over the year, and the rate for female veterans (5.0%) changed little.

» 36% were age 25 to 44, and 4% were age 18 to 24.

» Veterans with a service-connected disability had an unemployment rate of 4.8% in August 2016, about the same as veterans with no disability (4.7%).

» Nearly 1 in 3 employed veterans with a service-connected disability worked in the public sector in August 2016, compared with about 1 in 5 veterans with no disability.

» In 2016, the unemployment rate of veterans varied across the country, ranging from 1.8 percent in Indiana to 7.6 percent in the District of Columbia.

These numbers provide some good news. Male, female, and disabled vets are finding placement. But, you must drill down to see remaining concerns. For example, if 1 of 3 is employed in the public sector, the for-profit sector loses their potential.

The public sector transitions veterans into bureaucratic civil service and/or careers as first responders. These can certainly be reputable careers, even lucrative for some. Still, the transition to such systems is rarely competitive, and service positions support but do not drive the economy.

More important, competitive organizations miss the individual and group strengths of veterans. The University of Vermont lists the strengths arising from military service summarized here:[32]

» Leadership Training: The military trains people to accept and discharge responsibility for other people, for activities, for resources, and for one's own behavior.

---

32 (21 Strengths Arising From Military Experience)

» Ability to Work as a Team Member and Leader: Essential to the military experience is the ability to work as a member of a team. A good deal of military personnel serve as team leaders where they have analyzed situations and options, made appropriate decisions, given directions, followed through with a viable plan, and accepted responsibility for the outcome.

» Ability to Get Along with and Work with All Types of People: Military personnel have worked for and with people of all types of backgrounds, attitudes and characteristics. This experience has prepared service members and their families to work with all types of people on a continuing basis.

» Ability to Work Under Pressure and Meet Deadlines: Military personnel continuously set priorities, meet schedules, and accomplish their missions. Pressure and stress are built into this, but service members are taught how to deal with all these factors in a positive and effective manner.

» Ability to Give and Follow Directions: People in the military know how to work under supervision and can relate and respond favorably to others. They understand accountability for their actions and for their subordinates' actions.

» Systematic Planning and Organization: Most military operations require thorough planning and workload management. Carefully considered objectives, strengths and limitations of other people, resources, time schedules, supplies, logistics, and various other factors are always considered.

» Emphasis on Safety: Military safety training is among the best in the world. Service members understand the considerable cost in lives, property, and objectives when safety is ignored.

» Familiarity with Records and Personnel Administration: Service members are familiar with the necessity of keeping accurate records and completing all paperwork. There is always the requirement for accountability

» Ability to Conform to Rules and Structure: Individuals in the service have learned and followed rules every day in their working environment. While in this environment, they have also learned loyalty to their units and their leaders.

» Flexibility and Adaptability: All individuals in the service have learned to be flexible and adaptable to meet the constantly changing needs of any situation and mission. Last minute changes are common in any military or civilian working environment.

» Self-Direction: Many service members understand difficult and often complex issues and solve these issues or problems on the spot without systematic guidance from above.

» Initiative: Many military personnel can originate a plan of action or task to answer and solve many unusual problems regarding supplies, logistics, resources, and transportation.

» Work Habits: People in the military stay and finish their projects, a definite result of social maturity, integrity, determination, and self-confidence that they have learned, earned, and experienced in their military service.

» Global Outlook: Many people in the military have been stationed and served their country in various locations around the world. This residency and international experience have broadened their outlooks regarding customs, economies, languages and cultures of other countries.

» Client and Service-Oriented: Many military personnel are in the service industry. Their jobs are to facilitate, explain and expedite their patrons and client's needs, wants, and actions

» Specialized Advanced Training: All service personnel receive advanced training in their fields. Their career fields designate a specialized focus and skill building for their individual jobs. Advanced training and cross-referenced training can be in the computerized, financial, medical, engineering, administrative, personnel, technical, mechanical, and security fields.

The healthy employment rate for military veterans belies the fact that many veterans have been underemployed. With many in their early career stages and a dearth of statistics on their placement in mid-management and the c-suite, we lack evidence that they are recognized and rewarded as high-potential employees.

THE RISE OF LGBTQ EQUALITY

Other than issues of discrimination, corporations have not prioritized the hiring or development of members of the LGBTQ community. However, the Human Rights Campaign's Corporate Equality Index (CEI) for 2017 says, "The nation's largest employers have demonstrated through their actions that LGBTQQ people are not just tolerated, but welcomed in their workplaces and communities."[33]

Where employing LGBTQ members presents a difficulty for the employer, the employer has an ethical responsibility to step up and optimize talents and performance in the interest of shared goals. We cannot deny that social and cultural barriers remain a significant problem, but competitive businesses find it more difficult to hide behind such barriers, especially when they are positioned to influence and change things.

---

33 (Corporate Equality Index 2017: Rating Workplaces on Lesbian, Gay, Bisexual and Transgender Equality, 2017)

» The CEI's expectations of corporate behavior continue to evolve, but it based its 2017 ratings on the condition that "discrimination has no place in a top-rated CEI business."[34]

» Have sexual orientation and gender identity nondiscrimination protections explicitly included in all its operations, both within the U.S. and global operations.

» Require U.S. contractors to abide by companies' existing inclusive nondiscrimination policy.

» Implement internal requirements prohibiting U.S. company/law firm philanthropic giving to nonreligious organizations that have a written policy of discrimination based on sexual orientation and gender identity.

The CEI is demanding as you examine its expectations under these three principles. It pushes accountability down to supply chains and out to communities in comprehensive guidelines. And, meeting those metrics at 100% are the following:

1. Walmart Stores, Inc.
2. Exxon Mobil Corp.
3. Chevron Corp.
4. Berkshire Hathaway Inc.
5. Apple Inc.
6. General Motors Co.
7. Phillips 66
8. General Electric Co.
9. Ford Motor Co.
10. CVS Health Corp.
11. McKesson Corp.
12. AT&T Inc.
13. Valero Energy Corp.
14. UnitedHealth Group Inc.
15. Verizon Communications Inc.
16. AmerisourceBergen Corp.
17. Federal National Mortgage Association (Fannie Mae)
18. Costco Wholesale Corp.
19. HP Inc.
20. Kroger Co.

---

34 (Corporate Equality Index 2017: Rating Workplaces on Lesbian, Gay, Bisexual and Transgender Equality, 2017)

This list includes a variety of industry sectors including retail, automotive manufacturing, communications, healthcare, investment, and oil refining. It does not include aerospace, entertainment, light manufacturing, or hospitality. And, the internet is fast to identify "unfriendly" businesses.

A report by The Williams Institute at the UCLA School of Law sought to connect the presence of the LGBTQ community and business outcomes. Their results are summarized here:

» Strongest finding: LGBTQ-supportive policies or workplace climates are most strongly linked to more openness about being LGBTQ.

» Fairly strong findings: We see fairly strong links between LGBTQ-supportive policies and workplace climates to less discrimination, improved health outcomes, increased job satisfaction, and greater job commitment.

» Findings from a small number of studies: Other possible links between LGBTQ-supportive policies or workplace climates and improved workplace relationships, health insurance costs, creativity, and stock prices are not yet strong due to the small number of studies that assess these relationships.

» No studies: We have found no studies assessing possible links between LGBTQ-supportive policies or workplace climates and falling litigation costs, increased public sector customers, more individual consumers, and improved recruitment and retention.

» Connection to other research on business outcomes: Other research finds that these business outcomes which are influenced by LGBTQ-supportive policies or workplace lead to higher productivity and lower costs for employers, which in turn would enhance business profitability.[35]

35 (Lee Badgett & others, 2013)

The Williams Institute is a think tank devoted to studying issues affecting the LGBTQ community. They can only acknowledge the lack of research on the correlation between the presence of LGBTQ employees on the corporate bottom line. They do, however, see some demonstrative link between openness to LGBTQ members and beneficial social collateral like increased job satisfaction, job commitment, and improved healthcare outcomes.

If and to the extent that talent rules locating, hiring, and developing employees, it may reduce barriers to placement of high-potential employees who may belong to the LGBTQ community.

HIDDEN TALENTS AMONGST ALTERNATIVELY ABLED

Businesses are increasingly under compliance obligations with the evolving Americans with Disabilities Act. Their need to comply is not the issue here. Rather, we are interested in how organizations can discover and optimize the talent of alternatively abled people beyond the scope of federal and state legislation.

"In the past, being disabled prevented most of those so afflicted from even dreaming let alone fulfilling their most important goals and aspirations. However, as with most other traditional societal norms, this one is being put to the test by the Millennials."[36] Most Baby Boomers were born too long ago to take advantage of technology to offset their physical limitations. But, tech advances have helped already outspoken but disabled Millennials "have a realistic chance of getting their degrees, traveling, getting the jobs they want, and living as if there were nothing to hold them back."[37]

---

36 (Pisker, 2017)

37 (Pisker, 2017)

Because morbidity (the rate of disability) increases with age, disabilities are not perceived as a Millennials' problem. Even the *2016 Disability Statistics Annual Report* does not differentiate Millennials. "In 2015, of the US population with disabilities, over half (51.1%) were people in the working ages of 18-64, while 41.2% were 65 and older. Disability in children and youth accounted for only 7.2% (ages 5-17) and 0.4% (under 5 years old)."[38]

Even allowing for the failure to categorize Millennials, the report holds numbers in which we can see commonalities:

» In 2015, 34.9% of people with disabilities in the US ages 18-64 living in the community were employed compared to 76.0% for people without disabilities - a gap of 41.1 percentage points.

» The employment gap between those with a disability and those without has widened steadily over the past 8 years from 38.8 to 41.1 percentage points.

» There is state variation in the rates of employment for people with disabilities, from a high of 57.1% in Wyoming to a low of 25.4% in West Virginia; for people without disabilities, state employment rates ranged from a high of 83.8% in Minnesota to a low of 70.1% in Mississippi.

» In thirty states, the employment percentage gap between those with a disability and those without was 40 percentage points or greater; only three states showed an employment percentage gap less than 33.3 percentage points.

» Employment rates vary by type of disability. Employment rates are highest for people with hearing (51.0%) and vision disabilities (41.8%) and lowest for people with self-care (15.6%) and independent living disabilities (16.4%).[39]

---

38 (Kraus, 2017)

39 (Kraus, 2017)

The numbers argue that able disabled workers, talented workers are being overlooked for discovery, hire, and development. Businesses in compliance with A.D.A. begrudgingly comply with reasonable accommodation requirements, but few have proactive strategies for attracting, engaging, and retaining talented people with some physical limitations. We need to consider strategies to make that happen.

THE VALUE IN NUMBERS

Statistics have their value. But, they can be analytical without getting to a "truth." The fact is most studies of Millennials deal with the market they represent for products and services as the largest generation since the Baby Boomers.

That's not our interest here. Our focus remains on what their talent means to business innovation and productivity in a coinciding era of global competition. They are a force and a presence, and organizations will fast lose their edge if they do not act decisively and effectively to strategic policies and practices customized to their needs and expectations and aligned with corporate goals.

REFERENCES

21 Strengths Arising From Military Experience. (n.d.). Retrieved June 3, 2017 from University of Vermont: https://www.uvm.edu/~career/pdf/21_Strengths_Arising_From_Military_Experience_61670_7-1.pdf

(2016). *50 Best Workplaces for Diversity.* Fortune.

Age and Sex Composition: 2010 Census Briefs. (2011, May). Retrieved June 3, 2017 from census.gov: https://www.census.gov/prod/cen2010/briefs/c2010br-03.pdf

Allen, N. J. (1990). The measurement and antecedents of affective, continuance and normative commitment to the organization. *Journal of Occupational and Organizational Psychology , 63* (1), 1-18.

Ashgar, R. (2014, Jan 13). *What Millennials Want In The Workplace (And Why You Should Start Giving It To Them).* Retrieved May 16, 2017 from Forbes: https://www.forbes.com/sites/robasghar/2014/01/13/what-millennials-want-in-the-workplace-and-why-you-should-start-giving-it-to-them/#a95c7014c404

Aubrey, L. C. (2012, March 15). The Effect of Toxic Leadership. Carlisle, PA, USA: United States War College.

Berry, B. (2015, February 15). *An Interview with John Pendergast.* Retrieved April 10, 2017 from Conscious Variety: http://www.consciousvariety.com/articles/john-prendergast

Biggert, N. (1977). The Creative-Destructive Process of Organizational Change: The Case of the Post Office. *Administrative Science Quarterly , 22* (3), 16.

Bowman, J. (2015, May 14). *The Secret to PepsiCo, Inc.'s Success.* Retrieved January 13, 2017 from fool.com: http://www.fool.com/investing/general/2015/05/14/the-secret-to-pepsico-incs-success.aspx

Bruneau, M. (2016, May 26). *7 Behaviors of successful entrepreneurs.*

Retrieved June 18, 2016 from Forbes: http://www.forbes.com/sites/meganbruneau/2016/05/26/7-things-successful-entrepreneurs-do/#3a112991625b

Calvin, G. (2012, June 11). *Indra Nooyi's Pepsi challenge.* Retrieved January 13, 2017 from Hingam Schools.com: http://hpswebs.hingham-schools.com/hhs/teachers/sgeorge/pepsi%20article.pdf

Cilliza, C. (2015, Apr 30). *Millennials don't trust anyone. That's a big deal.* Retrieved May 16, 2017 from The Washington Post: https://www.washingtonpost.com/news/the-fix/wp/2015/04/30/millennials-dont-trust-anyone-what-else-is-new/?utm_term=.a2453525bffc

(2017). *Corporate Equality Index 2017: Rating Workplaces on Lesbian, Gay, Bisexual and Transgender Equality.* Washington, D.C: Human Rigths Campaign Foundation.

Dizikes, P. (2014, Oct 7). *Study: Workplace diversity can help the bottom line.* Retrieved June 4, 2017 from MIT News: http://news.mit.edu/2014/workplace-diversity-can-help-bottom-line-1007

Employment Situation of Veterans — 2016. (2017, March 22). Retrieved June 3, 2017 from Bureau of Labor Statistics: https://www.bls.gov/news.release/pdf/vet.pdf

Feeman, M. (2016). Rewriting the Self: History, memory, narrative. New York, New York, USA: Rutledge. Retrieved April 10, 2017 from https://books.google.com/books?hl=en&lr=&id=97tmCgAAQBAJ&oi=fnd&pg=PP1&dq=describe+the+human+condition+against+our+historical+memory&ots=3yNJT9qZ4z&sig=aqtcQlActVGRltpSmG--3Uafk47E#v=onepage&q&f=false

Flood, A. (2015). *The female millennial: a new era of talent.* PWC.

Fry, R. (2016, April 25). *Millennials overtake Baby Boomers as America's largest generation.* Retrieved June 3, 2017 from Pre Research: http://www.pewresearch.org/fact-tank/2016/04/25/millennials-overtake-baby-boomers/

Generational Breakdown: Info About All of the Generations. (n.d.). Retrieved June 3, 2017 from The Center for Generational Kinetics: http://genhq.com/faq-info-about-generations/

Gilbert, J. (2011, Sept/Oct). *The Millennials: A new generation of employees, a new set of engagement policies.* Retrieved June 3, 2017 from Ivey Business Journal: http://iveybusinessjournal.com/publication/the-millennials-a-new-generation-of-employees-a-new-set-of-engagement-policies/

Goldsmith. M. and Carter, L. (Ed.). (2010). *Best Practices in Talent Management: How.* San Francisco, CA, U.S.A.: John Wiley & Sons, Inc.

Green, A. (2015, February 2). *5 Ways Employers Discourage You From Negotiating Salary.* Retrieved May 16, 2016 from U.S. News Money: http://money.usnews.com/money/blogs/outside-voices-careers/2015/02/02/5-ways-employers-discourage-you-from-negotiating-salary

Harris, T. (1993, May-June). The Post-Capitalist Executive: An interview with Peter F. Drucker. *Harvard Business Review* .

Hebert, J. (26, Jan 2017). *Why Millennials Deserve More Respect at Work.* Retrieved May 13, 2017 from Fortune: http://fortune.com/2017/01/26/millennials-2/

Hofstrand, D. (2010, February). *Peter Drucker and Innovation.* From Iowa State University Extension and Outreach: http://www.extension.iastate.edu/agdm/wholefarm/html/c5-10.html

Howe, N. a. (2000). *Millenials are Rising: The Next Great Generation.* New York: Vintage.

Hudson, B. T. (1994, June). *Innovation through Acquistion.* Retrieved January 13, 2017 from The Cornell H.R.A. Quarterly: http://journals.sagepub.com/doi/pdf/10.1177/001088049403500318

Hunt, V. L. (2015, Jan). *Why diversity matters.* Retrieved June 3, 2017 from McKinsey & Company: http://www.mckinsey.com/business-functions/organization/our-insights/why-diversity-matters

"Pro-business," but expecting more: The Deloitte Millennial Survey 2017. (2017, May 13). From Deloitte: https://www2.deloitte.com/global/en/pages/about-deloitte/articles/millennial-survey-pro-business-but-expecting-more.html

Kaneshige, T. (2013, Oct 10). *Why Managers Need to Stop Worrying and Love Millennials.* Retrieved May 13, 2017 from CIO: http://www.cio.com/article/2381827/leadership-management/why-managers-need-to-stop-worrying-and-love-millennials.html

Kraus, L. (2017). *2016 Disability Statistics Annual.* University of New Hampshire. Durham, NH: Institute on Disability/UCED.

Lee Badgett, M., & others. (2013). *The Business Impact of LGBT-Supportive Workplace Policies.* Los Angeles: The Williams Institute.

Meyer, K. (2016, Jan 3). *Millennials as Digital Natives: Myths and Realities.* Retrieved May 14, 2017 from Neilsen Norman Group: https://www.nngroup.com/articles/millennials-digital-natives/

(2011). *Millennials at work: Reshaping the Workplace.* PWC.com.

Millennials in Adulthood: Detached from Institutions, Networked with Friends. (2014, March 7). Retrieved June 3, 2017 from Pew Research Center: http://www.pewsocialtrends.org/2014/03/07/millennials-in-adulthood/

Millennials: Confident. Connected. Open to Change. (2010, Feb 24). Retrieved May 13, 2017 from Pew Rsearch Center: Millennials: Confident. Connected. Open to Change

PepsiCo Earnings Preview: Snacks Could Offset Decline In Beverage Sales. (2014, February 11). Retrieved January 16, 2017 from Forbes: http://www.forbes.com/sites/greatspeculations/2014/02/11/pepsico-earnings-preview-snacks-could-offset-decline-in-beverage-sales/#7a-cac6e12d65

PepsiCo. (2016). *PepsiCo Reports Third Quarter 2016 Results*. PepsiCo.

Perna, M. (2016, Mar 5). *Millennials & Respect: Why It Matters So Much*. Retrieved May 16, 2017 from Linkedin: https://www.linkedin.com/pulse/millennials-respect-why-matters-so-much-mark-perna

Pisker, L. (2017, Jan 18). *Challenging Modern Society: Disabled Millennials*. Retrieved June 3, 2017 from Yout Time Magazine: http://www.youth-time.eu/articles-opinions/challenging-modern-society-disabled-millennials

Sasse, B. (2017). *The vanishing American Adult: Our Coming of Age Crisis - and How to Rebuid a Culture of Self-Reliance*. New York: St. Martin;s Press.

United States. (n.d.). Retrieved June 3, 2017 from Census Reporter: https://censusreporter.org/profiles/01000US-united-states/

Williams, T. (n.d.). *Racial Diversity: There's More Work to be Done in the Workplace*. Retrieved jUNE 3, 2017 from The Economist: https://execed.economist.com/blog/industry-trends/racial-diversity-there%E2%80%99s-more-work-be-done-workplace

Wilson, M. a. (2008). How Generational Theory Can Improve Teaching: Strategies for Working with the "Millennials". *Curresnts in Teaching and Learnng , 1* (1), 29-44.

Chapter 3

MULTI-TASKING AND MULTI-MODULE

A T SOME POINT, each generation creates its own image. Young people in the 1960s aggressively repudiated their parents' conservative haircuts and dress. The 1980s dressed them in athletic gear, baseball caps, and t-shirts with logos. Hip-hop and rap took over in the 90s. And, so on.

But, Millennials seem more fascinated by images and exploit the technology that helps define their character and style. Their behavior suggests an obsession with visual experiences and learning. They take and share selfies, display their lunches on social media, and dominate sites like Facebook, Instagram, Vine, and the latest app de jour.

They are heirs to the remark, falsely attributed to Andy Warhol, that everyone will be famous for 15-minutes.[40] Reality television is in their genes, and gaming and action films have accelerated their lives' narrative. Celebrity fascinates them, and romance and survival have been reduced to televised competitions.

The good and bad among Millennials have been taught and acculturated to learning in multiple modes. Chalk and talk systems fail

---

40   (Nuwer, 2014)

---

and disappoint them. They juggle, blend, and weave multiple inputs into volatile and dynamic cognitive experiences. They watch their music in videos, savor foods complexly, and stream experiences.

The Glossary of Multimodality explains, "Multimodality is an inter-disciplinary approach that understands communication and representation to be more than about language... Multimodal approaches have provided concepts, methods and a framework for the collection and analysis of visual, aural, embodied, and spatial aspects of interaction and environments, and the relationships between these."[41]

IT'S AN IMPROVISED LIFE

There is a certain hyperactivity about this. Millennials have been broadly labeled as showing attention deficit. The fact is they just do not live a linear life. They have left football and soccer to the "working" class. They prefer sports that emphasize spontaneity, improvisation, and individuality. Feeling no challenge from the predictable, they avoid plotted things in favor of dynamic things.

» Millennials court chaos convinced that there are resolutions, just as there are ends to their video games. They chased dragons through dungeons just for the exercise – also knowing they are not real.

» Millennials are part of socio-economic dialectic. A Nielsen survey remarks, "Having grown up amid growing media fragmentation, Millennials are hyper adept at multitasking and are fully immersed in both their digital and physical lives... They excel in a fast-paced world that requires an on-the-go lifestyle. They value, even demand, connectivity, convenience and options that allow them to be in control."[42]

---

41 (Modaity)
42 (The Keys to Unlocking the Millennial Mindset, 2016)

» Millennials feel they are engaged in change and capable of it. They believe systems and procedures have discoverable and achievable ends. And, their brains seek the paths and associates to achieve those ends. They like wins.

Millennials seem wired to prefer disruption because it creates its own dynamic and volatility. To them, the unsettled situation invites solution. They prefer enterprise and activity to status quo. The only standards of operation are those proven by test.

This best educated generation is not learned in traditional senses. Confident that everything they need to know is knowable, they assume it can be found. So, there is no need to immerse themselves in the canons of literature, history, and philosophy.

Continuity has not served them well in the first decades of this century. Dot.com crashes, economic recession, corrupt political leaders, and more reinforce a heritage of French Deconstructionist thinking. It makes all opinions equal and, therefore, none of them sure. Its denial of objectivity favors the subjectivity of impression. And, that has led to the diminishment of standards, values, and beliefs as continuing universals.

If "opinion" is the reasoned conclusion as close to confirmation as the evidence will permit, it is now dismissed as personal taste. Celebrity and acclaim have replaced authority. And, although logic is fundamental to the technology they use and respect, classical logic has little influence in conversation or discussion.

It follows, then, that millennials have put history in its place. Because they can find what they want on the internet, they do not have a deeper need to know. If they can find it or look it up, it must be true. Even if there are doubts about sources like Wikipedia, they are willing to accept its margin of error. And, even though they know better, they accept the content of the sites that rank high enough to land on first page of searches.

IS THIS A TURNING?

According the philosophers de jour, Neill Howe and William Strauss, Millennials are the unwitting participants of the latest "turning." Based on their study of American history, the authors delineated generations in approximately 20-year cycles – give or take a few years. Their work described parallel behaviors during those "generations."[43]

But, they then went on to turn the descriptive into predictive with followers attributing Nostradamus-like prophetic skills to them. Their influence has been enormous and decisive. But, critics like Rebecca Onion write, "The commercial success of this pseudoscientific mumbo-jumbo is irritating, but also troubling. The dominant US thinkers on the generational question tend to flatten social distinctions, relying on cherry-picked examples and reifying a vision of a 'society' that's made up mostly of the white and middle-class."[44]

Millennials are a presence and a force with many characteristics differentiating them from previous generations. But, it is bad history to see them as inevitable results of historical and economic forces any more than any other generation. Such dialectics depend on oversimplified stereotypes. Admittedly, "generational thinking is seductive, and for some of us it confirms our preconceived prejudices, but it's fatally flawed as a mode of understanding the world. Real life is not science fiction."[45]

Jessica Kriegel repeats the criticism of generational thinking, "If a generation were truly to be defined by the historical and cultural circumstances in which they were reared, then logic would have it that their defining traits would remain the same irrespective of age. Once frugal, always frugal; once family-oriented, always family-oriented."[46]

---

43 (Howe & Strauss, Generations: The History of America's Future, 1584 to 2069, 1991)
44 (Onion, 2015)
45 (Onion, 2015)
46 (Kriegel, 2015)

The Howe and Strauss methodology is like conspiracy theory. Their prophecy cannot be wrong because its "wrongness" is part of the prophecy. We can always see our present from a future perspective because we want to. It is the same intellectual dishonesty that lets people "identify" as something they are not. It is the bad logic that helps a white woman identify as black because she finds it fitting.

So, we must stop looking at Millennials as a single thing. Logic still holds fallacies in division and reification. No part speaks for the whole, and the whole is not true of all its members in the same way.

MILLENNIALS STRIVE FOR SELF TAUGHT SKILLS

Having warned against stereotyping people in the Millennial age grouping, we dare to say that they are generally heuristic. They have been educated in multimodal ways in family, school, church, and society. Where previous generations learned through memorization and drills, Millennials are so used to learning through sound, sight, and participation that they expect more. They learn best through sense stimulation.

Video games are not the cause of but a sign of their process. Gamification is heuristic. It asks players to pursue evolving goals while making fast and repeated decisions when encountering barriers. It is a "Super Mario" world where muscle memory synthesizes with other stimuli. It is a "Dungeons and Dragons" world where barriers are overcome with challenging cognitive analytics. It is a "Mortal Combat" world where fatality threatens agility.

They have learned to make fast decisions when challenged. And, they have responded by forging forward until moving to the side is a better option. Since early education, they have valued participation in threat free environments. Free to make mistakes, they grow in confidence that their forging forward will succeed.

There is no backward thinking in this pedagogy. History and other humanities become records of success and failure in forging ahead. Historic failures were basically inadequate skill or application. So, it is no surprise that millennials are drawn to technology where advances are incremental results of forging forward.

They are children of Nietzsche. And, "for Nietzsche the quest for truth became a search for honesty, which in turn became a question of who wills the truth."[47] They are not in search for *the* truth of gods, theologians, or philosophers. They find truth in the work or action they perform. Truth is their experience. "There is a clear sense of postmodernism... Nietzsche 'paves the way for a new kind of critique which would replace the matrix of truth and falsity with one of activity and reactivity, or affirmation and negation'."[48]

Millennials accept that many truths can exist simultaneously without priority or imbued value. Experience is their truth. Making things work is the means, and technology provides the tools. Progress is a moving forward, hitting a roadblock, and moving to the side to the gateway where they can move forward again.

Millennials are used to heuristic approaches to everything. "A heuristic is a strategy that ignores part of the information, with the goal of making decisions more quickly, frugally, and/or accurately than more complex methods."[49] They are most comfortable in projects managed as serial tasks with recognition and reward systems linked immediately to their task completion, just as video games celebrated with badges and bells and whistles.

This multimodal epistemology creates workers who "will carve out fresh concepts of public cyberspace and use information to empower

---

47   (Tilley, 2016)

48   (Tilley, 2016)

49   (Gierenzer & Gaissmaier, 2011, p. 54)

groups rather than individuals. As the first generation to grow up with mobile digital technology, Millennials expect nonstop interaction with their peers in forms that would have been unimaginable to prior generations of young adults. They will develop new standards for social networking, identifying a clear range of acceptable online attitudes and behaviors."[50]

But, as Kriegel points out, this inclination to heuristics is not indelible; "More important, generational stereotypes don't allow for natural human growth and development as people move from one life stage to another."[51] She asserts, "as anyone who has taken a basic logic or statistics course knows, correlation does not imply causation."[52]

A preference for heuristics does correlate with the generations attraction to technology. For one thing, "As media get highly interactive, multimodal, and navigable, the receiver tends to become the source of communication."[53] It is a brutal summary of S. Shyam Sundar's super analysis of the heuristic model, but the study indicates that young people assess credibility based on results. Rather than align process with idea or universal preconceptions, they assign credibility to things that have worked out.

This is an engineer's mindset, the belief that discovery and assemblage will produce desired results. It is an applied science focused on finding solutions to assigned tasks. The engineer relies heavily on a toolkit of methods, techniques, and scientific laws to build bridges, erect taller buildings, solve pollution problems, and develop computer applications. What marks this generation of designers and builders is an agility and an entrepreneur's interest in creative destruction.

---

50 (Howe & Strauss, The Next 20 Years: How Customer and Workforce Attitudes Will, 2007, p. 10)

51 (Kriegel, 2015)

52 (Kriegel, 2015)

53 (Sundar, 2008, p. 73)

THE DRAWBACKS

Any review of current literature insists Millennials present new problems in the workplace. Observers say, "Millennials have become the largest demographic in the workplace. But managers of all ages have struggled to find the best way to connect with a wave of twenty- and thirty-somethings who do most of their typing with their thumbs, work wearing earbuds, and claim they can hold meaningful conversations while monitoring five open browser windows."[54]

They claim, "Millennials and boomers find themselves in new territory regarding how to deal with each other. It is imperative for boomer managers to ensure the proper integration of the millennials into their organizational culture."[55]

One source even describes them through a list of quotations,[56] but the quotes say more about the manager than the employee:

» They do not care about customers.

» If you correct them, they quit.

» They think there is always an excuse that can make being late okay.

» They want a trophy just for showing up.

» Yelling and screaming is the only thing they understand.

» They pick up computer and cash register skills quickly, but if it breaks they cannot count back change from a $10 bill.

» She asked for an extended lunch hour to go shopping with her friends after her third day on the job.

» They assume it is okay to call me by my first name like we are buddies. I am their boss.

---

54 (Calvin, 2016)

55 (Calvin, 2016)

56 (Espinoza & Uklelja, 2016, p. 14)

» Anything extra nice I do, they act as if I owed it to them.

Describing the youngest of the generation, Bruce Tulgan says, The result is that those children of the 2000s simultaneously grew up way too fast and never grew up at all. They are privy to everything from a dangerously young age---their access to information, ideas, images, and sounds is completely without precedent. At the same time, they are isolated and scheduled to a degree that children never have been. Their natural habitat is one of physical atomization and relative inactivity, but total continuous connectivity and communication. They are used to feeling worldly and precocious--- highly engaged in a virtual peer ecosystem--- while enjoying the discourse at least of protection and direction from parents, teachers, and counselors.[57]

Forbes attributes the following workplace behaviors to Millennials (paraphrased here for brevity):[58]

» **Instant Gratification, Technology, Mentoring and a Need for Constant Feedback:** The immediacy of the social media technology has made it possible for them to interact almost instantaneously. Unlike Boomers who want their objectives and to be left alone to execute, they want an almost constant stream of feedback.

» **Forever in blue jeans**: Millennials are neither white or blue-collar workers. They want to work in jeans in casual dress at least once a week. Some gravitate to environments allowing shorts and t-shirts. The casual dress demonstrates their preference for blurring the lines between work and personal life.

» **Show me the money!** Most Millennial surveys claim to have little interest in money. They prefer satisfying and fulfilling work. But, these surveys are self-disclosing, and the respondents participate with some bias. For example, it is easy for well-paid tech workers

---

57 (Tulgan, 2013)

58 (Kiisel, 2012)

to minimize the importance of money, and few of them refuse the benefits of stock and profit sharing.

» **Give me transparency and a flat organization:** Millennials resent and resist traditional hierarchical organizations and command-and-control management methods.

THE POSITIVES

A Human Resources VP we know tells the story of a mid-manager who complained that a subordinate had no work ethic. The manager said, "She always leaves as soon as her shift is over. She never volunteers and never offers to take work home." The VP heard the manager out, but then pointed out that the woman worked two jobs and sent much of her income to family in Costa Rico. Her work ethic was not the problem, but the manager's handling of the employee was.

This immigrant's willingness to juggle multiple tasks with multiple responsibilities presents a management challenge. In a paper presented at the New Jersey Institute of Technology, Richard Sweeney lists behaviors of this multi-modal generation as positives worth managing correctly and productively. The list is repeated here with summarized explanations:

» **More Choices; More Selectivity:** "Millennials expect a much greater array of product and service selectivity. They have grown up with a huge array of choices and they believe that such abundance is their birthright."[59]

» **Experiential and Explanatory Learners:** Millennials do not read directions, preferring to learn by doing and interacting. Their gaming heritage offered prompt rewards and few penalties. They find lectures boring. "Millennials are more engaged through

---

59 (Sweeney, 2006, p. 2)

active learning, effective experiential processes such as games, case studies, hands-on experiences, and simulations that can speed their learning and hold their interest."[60]

» **Flexibility / Convenience:** "Millennials prefer to keep their time and commitments flexible longer... They want more granularity in the services so they can be interrupted and finish when they are ready without any loss or productivity."[61]

» **Impatience:** "Millennials, by their own admission, have no tolerance for delays. They expect their services instantly when they are ready. They require almost constant feedback to know how they are progressing. Their worst nightmare is when they are delayed, required to wait in line, or have to deal with some other unproductive process. Their desire for speed and efficiency cannot be overestimated."[62]

» **Personalization and Customization:** "Once Millennials do make their choices in products and services, they expect them to have as much personalization and customization features as possible to meet their changing needs, interests and tastes."[63]

» **Practical, Results Oriented:** "Millennials are interested in processes and services that work and speed their interactions. They prefer merit systems to others (e.g. seniority). Millennials are furious when they feel they are wasting their time; they want to learn what they have to learn quickly and move on."[64]

» **Multitaskers:** "Millennials excel at juggling several tasks at once since this an efficient, practical use of their time... They do want to use their time most efficiently and multitasking offers them more options."[65]

---

60 (Sweeney, 2006, p. 3)
61 (Sweeney, 2006, p. 3)
62 (Sweeney, 2006, p. 3)
63 (Sweeney, 2006, p. 3)
64 (Sweeney, 2006, p. 4)
65 (Sweeney, 2006, p. 4)

» **Digital Natives:** Millennials clearly adapt faster to computer and internet services because they have always had them... they expect the speed, convenience, flexibility and power provided by digitally provided services and resources."[66]

» **Gamers:** "Millennials have spent thousands of hours playing electronic, computer and video games. They love the constant interactivity, full motion multimedia, colorful graphics, the ability to learn and progress to higher levels, and the ability to collaborate with friends in their learning and competitions."[67]

» **Nomadic Communication Style:** "Millennials... are prolific communicators. They love and expect communication mobility; to remain in constant touch wherever and whenever, un-tethered. This is their firm desire to do whatever they need to do, obtain any services independent of their geography or distance."[68]

» **Media / Format Agnostic**: "Millennials most enjoy interactive full motion multimedia, color images, and audio although they can use any media, even text."[69]

» **Collaboration & Intelligence:** "After many years of collaborating at schools, day care, soccer teams, orchestras, peer-to peer networks, games, and other programmed activities, Millennials know how and when to work with other people more effectively. Even those who do not prefer collaboration typically do so, if they think it gives them a practical advantage."[70]

» **Balanced Lives:** "They don't want to work 80 hours a week and sacrifice their health and their leisure time, even for considerably higher salaries. Yet they expect to earn incomes exceeding their parents."[71]

---

66 (Sweeney, 2006, p. 4)
67 (Sweeney, 2006, p. 4)
68 (Sweeney, 2006, p. 5)
69 (Sweeney, 2006, p. 5)
70 (Sweeney, 2006, p. 5)
71 (Sweeney, 2006, p. 6)

» **Less Reading:** "Millennials, disturbingly, are not reading literature or newspapers as much as previous generations of the same
age. In fact, reading is down for most age groups but the decline
has been greatest among the youngest adult population. Certainly
this is caused in part by the increase in the competition from entertainment and educational options."[72]

» **Other Characteristics:** Millennials are "direct, often to the point
of appearing rude. They believe that they are all 'above average';
to be average is really to be mediocre. They are very confident,
perhaps because their Boomer parents constantly told them that
they would succeed at whatever they did."[73]

These Millennial behaviors reflect the author's university position
and perspective. He offers them as observations for fellow faculty. But,
the list describes behaviors as useful, valuable, and manageable.

MANAGING A NEW GENERATION

Best business practices call for the acceptance of millennials as
a forceful presence to be reckoned with. The sooner management
welcomes and embraces their value – and whatever unique behaviors go
with it, the more productive they can integrate that value in achievement
of organizational goals.

This chapter seeks to describe the management behavior that will
address issues created by millennials' multi-modal ways.

"Whether in their bedrooms, their dorm rooms, or their offices,
today's young people can do everything at the same time — text, game,
read an assignment, watch a sitcom, do research on Google, and keep

---

72   (Sweeney, 2006, p. 6)

73   (Sweeney, 2006, p. 6)

the TV on — without (apparently) missing a beat."[74]

Management must learn to design and monitor work with that in mind. The challenge to build work that is engaging in piece-work is enormous. The flexibility of white and no-collar work helps create engaging work. Regardless, the challenge is real and calls for a versatile management response.

» **Management must know the work**. They need immersion in the processes, metrics, and outcomes. Managers best understand work they have done themselves. Their hands and eyes remember the doing and can structure work that betters the work they have done.

Senior managers far removed from the work floor or processes are left to make decisions based on data, trends, and statistics.

» **Workers need a voice in the formation and measures of work.** They want choices and variety in their work. So, when management shows respect for the individual workers performance, they should have a say in its control and completion. Management profits from teaching people how to set goals more than it does in setting goals from the top.

Helping workers define and articulate accountability gives them ownership and responsibility for performance. Teaching them to identify, develop, test, and revise process brings incremental progress to the work. But, it also completes it enough to set new goals.

» **Training and development must deliver futures.** If a business has T&D capabilities, it must switch from teaching down; that is, it should shift from teaching compliance issues and corporate policy. Millennials need a sense of big pictures and their place in that vision.

---

74 (Howe & Nadler, Managing Millennials: How to Cope With a Generation of Multitaskers, 2010)

Any business should cover its exposure with information on safety, compliance, and risk management. But, T&D needs a new strategy that develops curricula on identifying high-potential employees and on organizational development that staffs the business's future.

» **Managers must strategize multitasking**. Work was once stable and stationary with workers performing within strict guidelines like timeclocks, piece work, and performance evaluations. In blue collar, white collar, or no collar work today, managers must structure work that encourages multi-tasking, work rotation, and experiential assignments.

The c-suite should review the structure of work. They must familiarize themselves with the work expected and how it affects corporate goals. If alignment is a corporate goal, senior executives must know what is going on. Executive input and feedback is at least as important as that of the workers themselves.

» **Quality onboarding is necessary.** Legacy hiring practices put new hires through an orientation program preoccupied with information on company policies and procedures. It has been a prophylactic approach by Human Resources to reduce compliance and safety risk. But, it needs to be so much more.

Onboarding should be an alignment process with time and quality enough allotted to acclimate new hires to culture, organization, and values. New hired Millennials prefer multi-modal access to those lessons, behaviors, and goals. They want to see, hear, and participate in the process. For Millennials, onboarding means "buy-in," and any accountability for such process respects that.

» **Performance is multi-modal.** Millennials generally do not do well in rote work. Sameness and routine are alien and discouraging for them. So, while all work cannot be customized to their individual needs, management is smart to create and revisit work to facilitate versatility in tools, planning, and execution.

Likewise, Millennials resent performance assessments that are templated and policy-driven. Software and app technology now makes performance assessment possible in real time across any number of devices. And, Millennials find that more engaging, helpful, and satisfying.

If Millennials are multi-modal by origin and inclination, all business can benefit from their habit of saying, "Why do it that way?" At their best, Millennials are telling management there are more sensible and productive ways to do things.

REFERENCES

21 Strengths Arising From Military Experience. (n.d.). Retrieved June 3, 2017 from University of Vermont: https://www.uvm.edu/~career/pdf/21_Strengths_Arising_From_Military_Experience_61670_7-1.pdf

(2016). *50 Best Workplaces for Diversity.* Fortune.

Age and Sex Composition: 2010 Census Briefs. (2011, May). Retrieved June 3, 2017 from census.gov: https://www.census.gov/prod/cen2010/briefs/c2010br-03.pdf

Allen, N. J. (1990). The measurement and antecedents of affective, continuance and normative commitment to the organization. *Journal of Occupational and Organizational Psychology , 63* (1), 1-18.

Ashgar, R. (2014, Jan 13). *What Millennials Want In The Workplace (And Why You Should Start Giving It To Them).* Retrieved May 16, 2017 from Forbes: https://www.forbes.com/sites/robasghar/2014/01/13/what-millennials-want-in-the-workplace-and-why-you-should-start-giving-it-to-them/#a95c7014c404

Aubrey, L. C. (2012, March 15). The Effect of Toxic Leadership. Carlisle, PA, USA: United States War College.

Berry, B. (2015, February 15). *An Interview with John Pendergast.* Retrieved April 10, 2017 from Conscious Variety: http://www.consciousvariety.com/articles/john-prendergast

Biggert, N. (1977). The Creative-Destructive Process of Organizational Change: The Case of the Post Office. *Administrative Science Quarterly , 22* (3), 16.

Bowman, J. (2015, May 14). *The Secret to PepsiCo, Inc.'s Success.* Retrieved January 13, 2017 from fool.com: http://www.fool.com/investing/general/2015/05/14/the-secret-to-pepsico-incs-success.aspx

Bruneau, M. (2016, May 26). *7 Behaviors of successful entrepreneurs.* Retrieved June 18, 2016 from Forbes: http://www.forbes.com/sites/meganbruneau/2016/05/26/7-things-successful-entrepreneurs-do/#3a112991625b

Calvin, G. (2012, June 11). *Indra Nooyi's Pepsi challenge.* Retrieved January 13, 2017 from Hingam Schools.com: http://hpswebs.hingham-schools.com/hhs/teachers/sgeorge/pepsi%20article.pdf

Calvin, G. (2016, Oct 21). *Three Big Mistakes Leaders Make When Managing Millennials.* Retrieved June 14, 2017 from Fortune: http://fortune.com/2016/10/21/millennials-workplace-management/

Cilliza, C. (2015, Apr 30). *Millennials don't trust anyone. That's a big deal.* Retrieved May 16, 2017 from The Washington Post: https://www.washingtonpost.com/news/the-fix/wp/2015/04/30/millennials-dont-trust-anyone-what-else-is-new/?utm_term=.a2453525bffc

Confidence in Institutions. (2016, June 5). Retrieved June 12, 2017 from Gallup.com: http://www.gallup.com/poll/1597/confidence-institutions.aspx

(2017). *Corporate Equality Index 2017: Rating Workplaces on Lesbian, Gay, Bisexual and Transgender Equality.* Washington, D.C: Human Rigths Campaign Foundation.

Dizikes, P. (2014, Oct 7). *Study: Workplace diversity can help the bottom line.* Retrieved June 4, 2017 from MIT News: http://news.mit.edu/2014/workplace-diversity-can-help-bottom-line-1007

Employment Situation of Veterans — 2016. (2017, March 22). Retrieved June 3, 2017 from Bureau of Labor Statistics: https://www.bls.gov/news.release/pdf/vet.pdf

Espinoza, C., & Uklelja. (2016). *Managing the Millennials: Discover the Core Competencies for Managing Today's Workforce* (2nd ed.). Hoboken, NJ: John Wiley & Sons.

Feeman, M. (2016). Rewriting the Self: History, memory, narrative. New York, New York, USA: Rutledge. Retrieved April 10, 2017 from https://books.google.com/books?hl=en&lr=&id=97tmCgAAQBAJ&oi=fnd&pg=PP1&dq=describe+the+human+condition+against+our+historical+memory&ots=3yNJT9qZ4z&sig=aqtcQlActVGRltpSmG--3Uafk47E#v=onepage&q&f=false

Flood, A. (2015). *The female millennial: a new era of talent.* PWC.

Fry, R. (2016, April 25). *Millennials overtake Baby Boomers as America's largest generation.* Retrieved June 3, 2017 from Pre Research: http://www.pewresearch.org/fact-tank/2016/04/25/millennials-overtake-baby-boomers/

Generational Breakdown: Info About All of the Generations. (n.d.). Retrieved June 3, 2017 from The Center for Generational Kinetics: http://genhq.com/faq-info-about-generations/

Gierenzer, G., & Gaissmaier, W. (2011). Heuristic Decision Making. *Annual Review of Psychology* , 451-481.

Gilbert, J. (2011, Sept/Oct). *The Millennials: A new generation of employees, a new set of engagement policies.* Retrieved June 3, 2017 from Ivey Business Journal: http://iveybusinessjournal.com/publication/the-millennials-a-new-generation-of-employees-a-new-set-of-engagement-policies/

Goldsmith. M. and Carter, L. (Ed.). (2010). *Best Practices in Talent Management: How.* San Francisco, CA, U.S.A.: John Wiley & Sons, Inc.

Green, A. (2015, February 2). *5 Ways Employers Discourage You From Negotiating Salary.* Retrieved May 16, 2016 from U.S. News Money: http://money.usnews.com/money/blogs/outside-voices-careers/2015/02/02/5-ways-employers-discourage-you-from-negotiating-salary

Harris, T. (1993, May-June). The Post-Capitalist Executive: An interview with Peter F. Drucker. *Harvard Business Review* .

Hebert, J. (26, Jan 2017). *Why Millennials Deserve More Respect at Work.* Retrieved May 13, 2017 from Fortune: http://fortune.com/2017/01/26/millennials-2/

Hofstrand, D. (2010, February). *Peter Drucker and Innovation.* From Iowa State University Extension and Outreach: http://www.extension.iastate.edu/agdm/wholefarm/html/c5-10.html

Howe, N. a. (2000). *Millenials are Rising: The Next Great Generation.* New York: Vintage.

Howe, N., & Nadler, R. (2010, Aug 25). *Managing Millennials: How to Cope With a Generation of Multitaskers.* Retrieved June 20, 2017 from eremedi.com: https://www.eremedia.com/tlnt/managing-millennials-how-to-cope-with-a-generation-of-multitaskers/

Howe, N., & Strauss, W. (1991). *Generations: The History of America's Future, 1584 to 2069.* New York: William Morrow & Company.

Howe, N., & Strauss, W. (2007, July-August). The Next 20 Years: How Customer and Workforce Attitudes Will. *Harvard Business Review* , 13.

Hudson, B. T. (1994, June). *Innovation through Acquistion.* Retrieved January 13, 2017 from The Cornell H.R.A. Quarterly: http://journals.sagepub.com/doi/pdf/10.1177/001088049403500318

Hunt, V. L. (2015, Jan). *Why diversity matters.* Retrieved June 3, 2017 from McKinsey & Company: http://www.mckinsey.com/business-functions/organization/our-insights/why-diversity-matters

"Pro-business," but expecting more: The Deloitte Millennial Survey 2017. (2017, May 13). From Deloitte: https://www2.deloitte.com/global/en/pages/about-deloitte/articles/millennial-survey-pro-business-but-expecting-more.html

Kaneshige, T. (2013, Oct 10). *Why Managers Need to Stop Worrying and Love Millennials*. Retrieved May 13, 2017 from CIO: http://www.cio.com/article/2381827/leadership-management/why-managers-need-to-stop-worrying-and-love-millennials.html

Kiisel, T. (2012, May 16). *Gimme, Gimme, Gimme -- Millennials in the Workplace*. Retrieved June 18, 2017 from Forbes: https://www.forbes.com/sites/tykiisel/2012/05/16/gimme-gimme-gimme-millennials-in-the-workplace/#738daed1bcea

Kraus, L. (2017). *2016 Disability Statistics Annual*. University of New Hampshire. Durham, NH: Institute on Disability/UCED.

Kriegel, J. (2015, May 29). *Why Generational Theory Makes No Sense*. Retrieved June 14, 2017 from Forbes.com: https://www.forbes.com/sites/oracle/2015/09/29/why-generational-theory-makes-no-sense/#156566678eaa

Lee Badgett, M., & others. (2013). *The Business Impact of LGBT-Supportive Workplace Policies*. Los Angeles: The Williams Institute.

McCord, P. (2014, Jan-Feb). *How Netflix Reinvented HR*. Retrieved June 21, 2017 from Harvard Business Review: https://hbr.org/2014/01/how-netflix-reinvented-hr

Meyer, K. (2016, Jan 3). *Millennials as Digital Natives: Myths and Realities*. Retrieved May 14, 2017 from Neilsen Norman Group: https://www.nngroup.com/articles/millennials-digital-natives/

(2011). *Millennials at work: Reshaping the Workplace*. PWC.com.

Millennials in Adulthood: Detached from Institutions, Networked with Friends. (2014, March 7). Retrieved June 3, 2017 from Pew Research Center: http://www.pewsocialtrends.org/2014/03/07/millennials-in-adulthood/

Millennials: Confident. Connected. Open to Change. (2010, Feb 24). Retrieved May 13, 2017 from Pew Rsearch Center: Millennials: Confident. Connected. Open to Change

Modaity. (n.d.). Retrieved June 12, 2017 from https://multimodalityglossary.wordpress.com/multimodality/

New Times for Multimodality? Confronting the Accountability Culture. (2012, May). *Journal of Adolescent & Adult Literacy* , 8.

Nuwer, R. (2014, April 8). *Andy Warhol Probably Never Said His Celebrated "Fifteen Minutes of Fame" Line.* Retrieved June 11, 2017 from Smithsonian Magazine: http://www.smithsonianmag.com/smart-news/andy-warhol-probably-never-said-his-celebrated-fame-line-180950456/

Onion, R. (2015, May 15). *Against generations.* Retrieved June 14, 2017 from AEON.com: https://aeon.co/essays/generational-labels-are-lazy-useless-and-just-plain-wrong

PepsiCo Earnings Preview: Snacks Could Offset Decline In Beverage Sales. (2014, February 11). Retrieved January 16, 2017 from Forbes: http://www.forbes.com/sites/greatspeculations/2014/02/11/pepsico-earnings-preview-snacks-could-offset-decline-in-beverage-sales/#7acac6e12d65

PepsiCo. (2016). *PepsiCo Reports Third Quarter 2016 Results.* PepsiCo.

Perna, M. (2016, Mar 5). *Millennials & Respect: Why It Matters So Much.* Retrieved May 16, 2017 from Linkedin: https://www.linkedin.com/pulse/millennials-respect-why-matters-so-much-mark-perna

Pisker, L. (2017, Jan 18). *Challenging Modern Society: Disabled Millennials.* Retrieved June 3, 2017 from Yout Time Magazine: http://www.youth-time.eu/articles-opinions/challenging-modern-society-disabled-millennials

Ponteriero, C. (2016, June 17). *11 institutions trusted more by millennials*. Retrieved June 12, 2017 from Property and Casuality 360°: http://www.propertycasualty360.com/2016/06/17/11-institutions-trusted-more-by-millennials

Sasse, B. (2017). *The vanishing American Adult: Our Coming of Age Crisis - and How to Rebuid a Culture of Self-Reliance*. New York: St. Martin;s Press.

Suarez, J. G. (2016, Nov 24). *A baby boomer's guide to managing millennials at work*. Retrieved June 12, 2017 from Los Angeles Times: http://www.latimes.com/business/la-fi-career-coach-boomers-millennials-20161124-story.html

Sundar, S. S. (2008). "The MAIN Model: A Heuristic Approach to Understanding Technology Effects on Credibility". (M. Flanagin, J. Metzge, & A. J., Eds.) *Digital Media* , 73-100.

Sweeney, R. (2006). Millennial Behaviors & Demographics. 1-10. Newark, NJ.

The Keys to Unlocking the Millennial Mindset. (2016, Sept. 8). Retrieved June 13, 2017 from Nielsen.com: http://www.nielsen.com/us/en/insights/news/2016/keys-to-unlocking-the-millennial-mindset.html

Tilley, P. W. (2016, June). Nietzsche's Perspectivism in Truth and Narrative. 1-13. Sidney, Australia.

Tulgan, B. (2013). *Meet Generation Z: The second generation within the giant "Millennial" cohort*. Retrieved June 18, 2017 from Rainmaker Thinking: http://www.rainmakerthinking.com/assets/uploads/2013/10/Gen-Z-Whitepaper.pdf

United States. (n.d.). Retrieved June 3, 2017 from Census Reporter: https://censusreporter.org/profiles/01000US-united-states/

Williams, T. (n.d.). *Racial Diversity: There's More Work to be Done in the Workplace*. Retrieved jUNE 3, 2017 from The Economist: https://

execed.economist.com/blog/industry-trends/racial-diversity-there%E2%80%99s-more-work-be-done-workplace

Wilson, M. a. (2008). How Generational Theory Can Improve Teaching: Strategies for Working with the "Millennials". *Curresnts in Teaching and Learnng*, 1 (1), 29-44.

Chapter 4

THE PRODUCT OF OUR ENVIRONMENT

THEIR CRITICS LABEL Millennials "The Me Me Me Generation[75]" and blame everything wrong on those participation trophies handed out at little league games.

Without conceding that there is anything uniquely self-centered about the Millennial generation, we do notice some patterns:

» The Millennial brand of self-importance often shows up as materialism.[76]

» They have come to equate looking good with feeling good, and to say that "we should do whatever makes us feel good or makes us happy."[77]

» "Most young people (62 percent) do not feel like adults when they turn 18. When asked to define adulthood in their own words, 'financial independence was their top response."[78]

---

75 (Stein, 2013)

76 (Twenge, 2006, p. 99)

77 (Twenge, 2006, p. 94)

78 (Bank of America/USA TODAY Better Money Habits® Report: Young Americans & Money, 2016, p. 3)

» "It's not so much that young adults are having trouble with adulting - they've simply redefined it."[79]

» Their work should not be just ... a way to make money, support a family, or gain social prestige but should provide a rich and fulfilling experience in and of itself. Jobs are no longer just jobs; they are lifestyle options."[80]

» "High levels of extraversion have been our adaptation: We are a generation with few shrinking violets."[81]

» "We gain self-esteem from our relationships with others, not from focusing on ourselves."[82]

» Despite their self-aggrandizing tendencies, narcissists feely say that they are not as moral or as likable as other people. They think they are better than others at most things, but are also fully aware that they're not very good at relationships. And no, it's not because narcissists are actually insecure underneath – there's no evidence of that."[83]

These same critical observers explain the apparent narcissism in endless opened pieces. They blame helicopter parenting, trophies for showing up, less disciplined schooling, modern music, reality television, and much more. But, "the real predictor of a shift toward a more me-first society was the change from blue-collar to white-collar jobs. This urbanization shift is tied up with the overall economic trend."[84]

The economic shift into which this generation was born and the economic recession during which they reached maturity has created conditions that channel their self-impression. For instance, their

79 Michelle Barlow qtd. in (Rebell, 2016)
80 (Twenge, 2006, p. 90)
81 (Twenge, 2006, p. 89)
82 (Twenge, 2006, p. 92)
83 (Twenge, 2006, pp. 92-93)
84 (Pappas, 2016)

continued life with their parents and late marriage age have become socio-economic norms that forestall financial security and alters perceptions of self-worth and achievable expectations.

What some call "disrespect" is partly a psychological self-defense, a self-assurance as much as anything else.

RESPECT IS A TWO-WAY STREET

"Respect is a value of all generations. How respect is understood is different though for each generation. For Boomers, respect is given to anyone who is an 'elder,' but for a Millennials, they are more likely to approach respect as something that goes both ways and is earned through behaviors, character, etc."[85]

Without the psychologists and the statistics, we can draw some common-sense conclusions:

» In various surveys, Millennials have self-identified as concerned about how they are perceived.

» They expect others to share their individual self-perception.

» Unlike preceding generations, they are less inclined to self-identify as a group or institution member. When asked to explain themselves, they are less likely to say that they are Roman Catholics, Republicans, or New Yorkers.

» They are more inclined to express themselves in terms of personal achievements. Having been told they can be anything they want to be, they will rattle off their resume.

» Others often overreact to their self-confidence as cocky and self-aggrandizing, but that's a misreading of their place in the maturing process. Where self-confidence is warranted, it is not conceit.

---

85 (What is Respect to a Millennial, a Boomer, and a Gen X'er?, 2016)

» Others confuse self-confidence with self-interest, and self-possession with selfishness.

Still, understood or not, these behaviors present management with challenges demanding a new kind of attention. That is, managements discipline will not likely change the traits. So, we should look for reconfigured ways to approach, assess, and assimilate the behaviors.

MILLENNIALS ARE OUTSPOKEN

Millennials are used to collaborating in teams or projects in which they are encouraged to speak out. They may not consider their input important or vital, but they expect it to be treated as equal to or equal with that of others.

If their wish to participate and speak up is deemed precocious and precious by others, that resentment says more about the critics than about the Millennials themselves. Too many established employees think they own the work. Their reluctance to change conflicts with their criticism of what they consider the Millennials sense of entitlement.

Where the conflicts are clear and public, management needs to resolve them clearly with retraining and dialog. Too many companies allow ghosts to proliferate and haunt. An HR director I know tells a story of his attempt to arrange an awards and recognition event only to have a series of people insist that he could not hold it there because the last time they met there, layoffs were announced. When he proposed another location, people told him that the last event held there led to a fight between workers. And, so the ghosts of events past kept cropping up.

He recommends that when established workers complain about Millennial behaviors, we should first look at the openness and willingness of the established employees. So, here's some habits you can build:

» Millennials don't like to be surprised when they feel something has been kept from them. They expect to play on level fields, so put everything on the table.

» Like an annoying toddler, they want to know why. And, they will ask "why?" repeatedly until they are satisfied. However, you can look at "why" as a call-to-order. It calls on you to revisit the casualty and justification for systems. If process is clear, they won't ask "why?"

» They do not like to hear, "You can't do that!" or "That won't work?" And, their retort, "Why not?" is a challenge to the business to better itself.

» When management positions established workers and mentor pros as information centers, living kiosks, they become the go-to information providers and shed the "senior" label.

» Millennials want recognition regularly and promptly, but management strikes an important note when it encourages and leverages peer testimonials.

» Management and established workers should enjoy their work. The enjoyment does not come in the form of lavish perks, parties, and pastries. But, workers who show satisfaction and confidence in their process and outcomes have a positive influence on others.

If they seem outspoken, you may not be listening. True, they have little positive experience with hierarchical cultures that would define their "place." True, they may benefit from a more sensitive conversational approach. And, true, they should learn that their taste in things does not approach the value of thoughtfully reached opinion.

But, Millennial social errors should not diminish their contribution. That apparent disrespect is energy waiting to be harnessed.

THE THEORY OF MILLENNIAL ENTITLEMENT

Grandparents have been calling their progeny "spoiled" throughout recorded history. "Entitled" has been used so frequently it has no meaning. We are indebted to the French sociologist Pierre Bourdieu's work throughout the 20th century. His concept of "habitus" sought a commonsense description that would encompass a generation's practical behavior, a sense of the social property that directs but does not determine its behavior.

"In essence, habitus captures a particular collective's shared set of understandings, expectations, and embodied postures toward the world. It encompasses cognitive elements (e.g., stocks of knowledge, perceptions, attitudes and tastes) social elements (e.g., modes of interaction), and behavioral/corporal elements (e.g., ways of walking and talking) that are characteristic of a particular social group."[86]

In part, we reap what we sow. Before you write off Millennials for wanting instant satisfaction or trophies for showing up, you should remember who taught and trained them. "The Baby Boomers were singled out as a special generation, and they have instilled this same sense of self in their children, offering continuous self-reinforcement, emphasizing the special and unique status of their children and focusing on the importance of building self-esteem."[87]

MILLENNIALS ARE EMPOWERED

Millennials were born into a brave new world where history had lost its social value in favor of everything *au currant*. The access to digital information spread fads and celebrity, distorted opinion and validity, and empowered the global population.

---

86   (Allen, Allen, Karl, & White, 2015, p. 16)
87   (Allen, Allen, Karl, & White, 2015, p. 17)

"Millennials have come of age in a world with unprecedented access to people as well as nearly instant acquisition of information and goods. Access to people is an email or text away. Finding answers to questions only requires typing in a search word."[88] Goods are readily accessed, and many are free. Sharing is no longer transactional; it is merely a transmission. People communicate on a plane not up or down a hierarchy. And, the impressive power of social media tools has democratized information often at the expense of intelligence. Playing fields have been leveled, and digital reviews have undermined authorities. In short, the digital age has enabled continuous self-presentation.

In Bourdieu's terms, they act with the "body" of their generation. Critics have scrutinized his theories ad nauseum, but "he has opened up the possibility of a type of sociological explanation that is at once inter-disciplinary (combining among other disciplines sociology, philosophy, history, psychology and linguistics), rigorous and comprehensive, and which takes sociological theorizing beyond the boundaries traditionally assigned to it."[89]

His key contribution may lie in his placing habitus in a phenomenological context. That is, phenomenology had greatly influenced the intellectual community that preceded and welcomed the Millennials. With its assumption of co-existence and co-dependency, it contributed to the socio-historical climate into which Millennials grew.

Their lives have been marked by international terrorism, unresolved racial issues, serial economic upheavals, costly failures among the "too big to fail" corporations, insidious betrayals by religious leaders, and rapacious ethical practices by corporate and government leaders. Their ancestors have hardly been models of behavior. A lot of the elders' institutions simply do not deserve respect.

---

88   (Allen, Allen, Karl, & White, 2015, pp. 17-18)
89   (Lizardo, 2004, p. 395)

Dying with those social values is the distrust for hierarchy and meritocracy. "Millennials are skeptical of 'paying their dues' due to the mistrust between employer and employee that they've witnessed first-hand in their parents' situations. Thus, Millennials approach their career like free agents, taking ownership and looking for new opportunities or creating their own through entrepreneurship."[90]

The habitus we label Baby Boomers has difficulty grasping this independence and ambition. The Boomers confuse empowerment with the social entitlements that have been institutionalized during the same years. They confuse empowerment with demand and expectation for government handouts.

Millennials have little interest in living up to some idea of the past. Unless they are immigrants they do not worry about rocking the boat. As very in-the-moment personalities, they want ownership, equity, legacy, and impact now – not at retirement.

So, it follows that they are anxious to move forward and feel empowered to find the culture and place where that can happen. Responsible for enormous education debt and stunned by reversals in their parents' financial security, they feel empowered to dictate and manage their personal micro-economy. And, their historical sense of equity with and superiority to peers fills them with optimism and confidence that all problems can be solved.

THE 'SMARTER' GENERATION

Not since the Renaissance has a generation found itself so far ahead of its heritage in the mastery of new knowledge and skills. "Today's young adults (Millennials ages 18 to 33 in 2014) are much better educated than the Silent generation."[91] Millennials have accumulated more college

---

90   (Jenkins, 2017)
91   (Patten & Fry, 2015)

level credits than previous generations, but the quality of the learning leaves something to be desired.

They have a quantity of exposure that is different from learning. *Exposure to* is not necessarily *education in*. Their technological adeptness at finding and exploiting shortcuts gets them through much learning process in a world where the volume of exposure is so great no one could reasonably be expected to process.

"Media exposure has taught these young people to challenge any tradition, institution, value, or person they choose, and in many respects they are confused by media-highlighted scandal and dishonesty in industry and the government. They have seen a meteoric rise in stock prices and grew up in a world of cell phones, pagers, the Internet, and the Web. Millennials take class notes on personal digital assistants, get their information from blogs and wikis, and are asked by their professors to turn off their cell phones in their facetoface courses."[92]

Because they have unprecedented access to global events, they capture visuals filtered by media formats and political views. And, while Millennials are the most diverse generation in history, they share a homogenized character. It's different enough from their parents' generation's homogenization to be noticeable, but there is considerable standardization their habitus would not admit.

Still, what's new about their knowledge, skills, and abilities challenges previous learners, especially in the workplace. "They can complete a task, listen to the portable CD player [Notice how dated this reference is], and talk on the cell phone simultaneously, but employers report that their basic skill levels, critical thinking ability, and initiative are developmentally lacking. Millennials bring a mindset and approach to the workplace and the world community that many simply cannot comprehend."[93]

---

92   (Dziuban, Moskal, & Hartman, n.d., p. 3)

93   (Dziuban, Moskal, & Hartman, n.d., p. 4)

MILLENNIALS LEARNED DIFFERENTLY

Millennials may seem smarter because they are smarter differently. Having aged through a world of war, recession, divorce, and other disappointments, their achievement is noteworthy. They do like immediate recognition and reward, but they have the confidence to enjoy life. They are far more sociable than given credit for and extremely tolerant of diversity at all levels. Realistic and competitive, they remain spiritual and optimistic overall.[94]

At their most ambitious, Millennials expect direction on focus and project management. Collaborative as they are, they need some organizational direction. Having always lived with computers, they underestimate their addiction and refuse to let it interfere with a felt independence. Tied to computers, they trust the tools to make all changes necessary. With an engineering discipline, they assume all problems are solvable - or irrelevant.[95]

And, as collaborators, they are fiercely loyal to peers, parents, and possibilities. They believe the most difficult problems come down to stacking Legos®, Tetris® blocks, and Minecraft® Mods. And, trophies, badges, and tokens prove their progress.

Millennials were not born with technology skills, but they arrived in kindergarten with fast hardening aptitude. They learned how to use tech from friends and older siblings. And, they regularly seek help from those they know have superior strengths.

The fact is, Millennials do respect their elders, but they also expect to be treated as equals. And, the generations that manage them seem to have a problem with that. "It boils down to listening seriously to the other person's perspective, avoiding high-handed treatment that underscores

---

94 (Generational Differences Chart, n.d.)
95 (Generational Differences Chart, n.d.)

the recipient's inferior/dependent position, making decisions based on consensus rather than arbitrary opinions, and believing that the other person has valuable contributions to make."[96]

While Millennials are the most educated generation, they have not proven strongly literate. While they have proven creative in service of visual arts, you will find most of the creativity in gaming, content, marketing, and technology. They have been raised on blended learning and see no value in chalk-and-talk training. Learning must be reciprocal, must offer a challenge, and have some clear "what's in it for me."

They have little regard for the authenticity of the past. The past is done and offers nothing realizable. Without a past, they lack sentimentality. They have no need to know the history at Ford or GE when only their present is effectively important. So, they measure quality employment on the strength and ethics of its leaders.

Older workers see such behaviors, misread them, and resist a better understanding, and that intelligence gap can make management difficult.

PRACTICAL BUSINESS SOLUTIONS

The perception gap between Millennials and older workers is significant enough that, without sustained management, it will repress innovation, entrench legacy thinking, and prove counterproductive. The best companies have been addressing it for some time, and they seem to understand this is a journey.

Senior workers need help in adjusting to new needs. Even the older Millennials find themselves well behind the youngest. Still, these workers offer the most accessible and ready tool to creating a positive workforce.

---

96 (Perna, 2016)

» The established workers appreciate regular and immediate recognition. They welcome the termination of the drudgery of the annual performance appraisal.

» They find personal respect in acknowledgement for new work and for feedback integrated.

» Management can optimize the contributions of legacy workers by developing them as effective mentors on corporate culture and expectations as well as process and technique.

» One way to do this is to divorce expertise from metrics and communicate it in terms of goals and values alignment.

» The mindset and mental model of the more senior employees needs re-engineering, and that assumes the presence of a knowing and committed executive leadership.

» **New Hires** need a sense of a place for their value from the earliest stage of recruitment. Keys to their tenure and longevity lie in the felt respect as a continuing dynamic.

» Recruiting must address issues of core values as well as the knowledge, skills, and abilities in which they have such confidence.

» Sophisticated testing can identify the most productive match in terms of emotional intelligence.

» Millennial recruits want work designed to allow flexibility and life/work balance as it reconfigures the work of older workers.

» They need a full and lengthy onboarding process that may last up to three years as one sign of the career path they want to visualize.

» Everyone benefits from reverse mentoring when they are encouraged to introduce older peers to what they bring to the operation.

» And, they put more value on job perks that align with corporate vision rather than competitive frills. For example, they pay more respect to a benefit that might allow them creative time than to a free lunch.

» Leadership must drive a culture of psychological safety where voices are encouraged and recognized.

The management solution lies in creating a blended, purpose-driven climate where work is synonymous with outcomes, where it serves higher values, and pictures an achievable career path.

REFERENCES

21 Strengths Arising From Military Experience. (n.d.). Retrieved June 3, 2017 from University of Vermont: https://www.uvm.edu/~career/ pdf/21_Strengths_Arising_From_Military_Experience_61670_7-1.pdf

(2016). *50 Best Workplaces for Diversity.* Fortune.

Age and Sex Composition: 2010 Census Briefs. (2011, May). Retrieved June 3, 2017 from census.gov: https://www.census.gov/prod/cen2010/ briefs/c2010br-03.pdf

Allen, N. J. (1990). The measurement and antecedents of affective, continuance and normative commitment to the organization. *Journal of Occupational and Organizational Psychology , 63* (1), 1-18.

Allen, R., Allen, D., Karl, K., & White, C. (2015). Are Millennials Really an Entitled Generation? An Investigation into. *Jounral of Business Diversity , 15* (2), 14-26.

Are Millennials Really Narcissists? (2016, July 31). Retrieved July 22, 2017 from neuroamer.com: https://neuroamer.com/2016/07/31/ are-millennials-really-narcissists-lets-look-at-data/

Ashgar, R. (2014, Jan 13). *What Millennials Want In The Workplace (And Why You Should Start Giving It To Them).* Retrieved May 16, 2017 from Forbes: https://www.forbes.com/sites/robasghar/2014/01/13/ what-millennials-want-in-the-workplace-and-why-you-should- start-giving-it-to-them/#a95c7014c404

Aubrey, L. C. (2012, March 15). The Effect of Toxic Leadership. Carlisle, PA, USA: United States War College.

(2016). *Bank of America/USA TODAY Better Money Habits® Report: Young Americans & Money.* Bank of America/USA Today.

Berry, B. (2015, February 15). *An Interview with John Pendergast.* Retrieved April 10, 2017 from Conscious Variety: http://www.con- sciousvariety.com/articles/john-prendergast

Biggert, N. (1977). The Creative-Destructive Process of Organizational Change: The Case of the Post Office. *Administrative Science Quarterly , 22* (3), 16.

Bowman, J. (2015, May 14). *The Secret to PepsiCo, Inc.'s Success.* Retrieved January 13, 2017 from fool.com: http://www.fool.com/investing/general/2015/05/14/the-secret-to-pepsico-incs-success.aspx

Bruneau, M. (2016, May 26). *7 Behaviors of successful entrepreneurs.* Retrieved June 18, 2016 from Forbes: http://www.forbes.com/sites/meganbruneau/2016/05/26/7-things-successful-entrepreneurs-do/#3a112991625b

Calvin, G. (2012, June 11). *Indra Nooyi's Pepsi challenge.* Retrieved January 13, 2017 from Hingam Schools.com: http://hpswebs.hingham-schools.com/hhs/teachers/sgeorge/pepsi%20article.pdf

Calvin, G. (2016, Oct 21). *Three Big Mistakes Leaders Make When Managing Millennials.* Retrieved June 14, 2017 from Fortune: http://fortune.com/2016/10/21/millennials-workplace-management/

Cilliza, C. (2015, Apr 30). *Millennials don't trust anyone. That's a big deal.* Retrieved May 16, 2017 from The Washington Post: https://www.washingtonpost.com/news/the-fix/wp/2015/04/30/millennials-dont-trust-anyone-what-else-is-new/?utm_term=.a2453525bffc

Confidence in Institutions. (2016, June 5). Retrieved June 12, 2017 from Gallup.com: http://www.gallup.com/poll/1597/confidence-institutions.aspx

(2017). *Corporate Equality Index 2017: Rating Workplaces on Lesbian, Gay, Bisexual and Transgender Equality.* Washington, D.C: Human Rigths Campaign Foundation.

Dizikes, P. (2014, Oct 7). *Study: Workplace diversity can help the bottom line.* Retrieved June 4, 2017 from MIT News: http://news.mit.edu/2014/workplace-diversity-can-help-bottom-line-1007

Dziuban, C., Moskal, P., & Hartman, J. (n.d.). Higher Education, Blended Learning and the Generations: Knowledge is Power No More.

Employment Situation of Veterans — 2016. (2017, March 22). Retrieved June 3, 2017 from Bureau of Labor Statistics: https://www.bls.gov/news.release/pdf/vet.pdf

Espinoza, C., & Uklelja. (2016). *Managing the Millennials: Discover the Core Competencies for Managing Today's Workforce* (2nd ed.). Hoboken, NJ: John Wiley & Sons.

Feeman, M. (2016). Rewriting the Self: History, memory, narrative. New York, New York, USA: Rutledge. Retrieved April 10, 2017 from https://books.google.com/books?hl=en&lr=&id=97tmCgAAQBAJ&oi=fnd&pg=PP1&dq=describe+the+human+condition+against+our+historical+memory&ots=3yNJT9qZ4z&sig=aqtcQlActVGRltpSmG--3Uafk47E#v=onepage&q&f=false

Flood, A. (2015). *The female millennial: a new era of talent.* PWC.

Fry, R. (2016, April 25). *Millennials overtake Baby Boomers as America's largest generation.* Retrieved June 3, 2017 from Pre Research: http://www.pewresearch.org/fact-tank/2016/04/25/millennials-overtake-baby-boomers/

Gabbard, G. O. H. (2016). The many faces of narcissism. *World Psychiatry , 15* (2), 115-116.

Generational Breakdown: Info About All of the Generations. (n.d.). Retrieved June 3, 2017 from The Center for Generational Kinetics: http://genhq.com/faq-info-about-generations/

Generational Differences Chart. (n.d.). WMFC.org.

Gierenzer, G., & Gaissmaier, W. (2011). Heuristic Decision Making. *Annual Review of Psychology , 451-481.*

Gilbert, J. (2011, Sept/Oct). *The Millennials: A new generation of employees, a new set of engagement policies.* Retrieved June 3, 2017 from

Ivey Business Journal: http://iveybusinessjournal.com/publication/the-millennials-a-new-generation-of-employees-a-new-set-of-engagement-policies/

Goldsmith. M. and Carter, L. (Ed.). (2010). *Best Practices in Talent Management: How.* San Francisco, CA, U.S.A.: John Wiley & Sons, Inc.

Green, A. (2015, February 2). *5 Ways Employers Discourage You From Negotiating Salary.* Retrieved May 16, 2016 from U.S. News Money: http://money.usnews.com/money/blogs/outside-voices-careers/2015/02/02/5-ways-employers-discourage-you-from-negotiating-salary

Harris, T. (1993, May-June). The Post-Capitalist Executive: An interview with Peter F. Drucker. *Harvard Business Review* .

Hebert, J. (26, Jan 2017). *Why Millennials Deserve More Respect at Work.* Retrieved May 13, 2017 from Fortune: http://fortune.com/2017/01/26/millennials-2/

Hofstrand, D. (2010, February). *Peter Drucker and Innovation.* From Iowa State University Extension and Outreach: http://www.extension.iastate.edu/agdm/wholefarm/html/c5-10.html

Howe, N. a. (2000). *Millenials are Rising: The Next Great Generation.* New York: Vintage.

Howe, N., & Nadler, R. (2010, Aug 25). *Managing Millennials: How to Cope With a Generation of Multitaskers.* Retrieved June 20, 2017 from eremedi.com: https://www.eremedia.com/tlnt/managing-millennials-how-to-cope-with-a-generation-of-multitaskers/

Howe, N., & Strauss, W. (1991). *Generations: The History of America's Future, 1584 to 2069.* New York: William Morrow & Company.

Howe, N., & Strauss, W. (2007, July-August). The Next 20 Years: How Customer and Workforce Attitudes Will. *Harvard Business Review* , 13.

Hudson, B. T. (1994, June). *Innovation through Acquistion.* Retrieved January 13, 2017 from The Cornell H.R.A. Quarterly: http://journals. sagepub.com/doi/pdf/10.1177/001088049403500318

Hunt, V. L. (2015, Jan). *Why diversity matters.* Retrieved June 3, 2017 from McKinsey & Company: http://www.mckinsey.com/busi-ness-functions/organization/our-insights/why-diversity-matters

"Pro-business," but expecting more: The Deloitte Millennial Survey 2017. (2017, May 13). From Deloitte: https://www2.deloitte.com/glob-al/en/pages/about-deloitte/articles/millennial-survey-pro-busi-ness-but-expecting-more.html

Jenkins, R. (2017, August 7). *Why Millennials Are So Entitled (Parents Are Partly Blamed).* Retrieved August 29, 2017 from Inc.: https://www. inc.com/ryan-jenkins/this-is-why-millennials-are-entitled.html

Kaneshige, T. (2013, Oct 10). *Why Managers Need to Stop Worrying and Love Millennials.* Retrieved May 13, 2017 from CIO: http://www. cio.com/article/2381827/leadership-management/why-managers-need-to-stop-worrying-and-love-millennials.html

Kiisel, T. (2012, May 16). *Gimme, Gimme, Gimme -- Millennials in the Workplace.* Retrieved June 18, 2017 from Forbes: https://www.forbes. com/sites/tykiisel/2012/05/16/gimme-gimme-gimme-millenni-als-in-the-workplace/#738daed1bcea

Kraus, L. (2017). *2016 Disability Statistics Annual.* University of New Hampshire. Durham, NH: Institute on Disability/UCED.

Kriegel, J. (2015, May 29). *Why Generational Theory Makes No Sense.* Retrieved June 14, 2017 from Forbes.com: https://www. forbes.com/sites/oracle/2015/09/29/why-generational-theo-ry-makes-no-sense/#156566678eaa

Lee Badgett, M., & others. (2013). *The Business Impact of LGBT-Sup-portive Workplace Policies.* Los Angeles: The Williams Institute.

Lizardo, O. (2004). The Cognitive Origins of Bourdieu's Habitus. *Journal for the Theory of Social Behaviour 34:4 , 34* (4), 375-401.

McCord, P. (2014, Jan-Feb). *How Netflix Reinvented HR*. Retrieved June 21, 2017 from Harvard Business Review: https://hbr.org/2014/01/how-netflix-reinvented-hr

Meyer, K. (2016, Jan 3). *Millennials as Digital Natives: Myths and Realities*. Retrieved May 14, 2017 from Neilsen Norman Group: https://www.nngroup.com/articles/millennials-digital-natives/

(2011). *Millennials at work: Reshaping the Workplace*. PWC.com.

Millennials in Adulthood: Detached from Institutions, Networked with Friends. (2014, March 7). Retrieved June 3, 2017 from Pew Research Center: http://www.pewsocialtrends.org/2014/03/07/millennials-in-adulthood/

Millennials: Confident. Connected. Open to Change. (2010, Feb 24). Retrieved May 13, 2017 from Pew Rsearch Center: Millennials: Confident. Connected. Open to Change

Modaity. (n.d.). Retrieved June 12, 2017 from https://multimodalityglossary.wordpress.com/multimodality/

New Times for Multimodality? Confronting the Accountability Culture. (2012, May). *Journal of Adolescent & Adult Literacy* , 8.

Nuwer, R. (2014, April 8). *Andy Warhol Probably Never Said His Celebrated "Fifteen Minutes of Fame" Line*. Retrieved June 11, 2017 from Smithsonian Magazine: http://www.smithsonianmag.com/smart-news/andy-warhol-probably-never-said-his-celebrated-fame-line-180950456/

Onion, R. (2015, May 15). *Against generations*. Retrieved June 14, 2017 from AEON.com: https://aeon.co/essays/generational-labels-are-lazy-useless-and-just-plain-wrong

Pappas, S. (2016, Feb 8). *Why Are Millennials Narcissistic? Blame Income Inequality.* Retrieved July 20, 2017 from LiveScience.com: https://www.livescience.com/53635-why-millennials-are-narcissistic.html

Patten, E., & Fry, R. (2015). *How Millennials today compare with their grandparents 50 years ago.* Pew Research Center.

PepsiCo Earnings Preview: Snacks Could Offset Decline In Beverage Sales. (2014, February 11). Retrieved January 16, 2017 from Forbes: http://www.forbes.com/sites/greatspeculations/2014/02/11/pepsico-earnings-preview-snacks-could-offset-decline-in-beverage-sales/#7acac6e12d65

PepsiCo. (2016). *PepsiCo Reports Third Quarter 2016 Results.* PepsiCo.

Perna, M. (2016, Mar 5). *Millennials & Respect: Why It Matters So Much.* Retrieved May 16, 2017 from Linkedin: https://www.linkedin.com/pulse/millennials-respect-why-matters-so-much-mark-perna

Pisker, L. (2017, Jan 18). *Challenging Modern Society: Disabled Millennials.* Retrieved June 3, 2017 from Yout Time Magazine: http://www.youth-time.eu/articles-opinions/challenging-modern-society-disabled-millennials

Ponteriero, C. (2016, June 17). *11 institutions trusted more by millennials.* Retrieved June 12, 2017 from Property and Casuality 360°: http://www.propertycasualty360.com/2016/06/17/11-institutions-trusted-more-by-millennials

Rebell, R. (2016, Oct 10). *RPT-COLUMN-For millennials, adulthood now defined by financial freedom.* Retrieved July 22, 2017 from Reuters.com: http://www.reuters.com/article/column-money-adulthood-repeat-column-per-idUSL1N1CG1AS?type=companyNews

Sasse, B. (2017). *The vanishing American Adult: Our Coming of Age Crisis - and How to Rebuid a Culture of Self-Reliance.* New York: St. Martin;s Press.

Stein, J. (2013, May 20). *MIllennials: The Me Me Me Generation*. Retrieved July 22, 2017 from Time.com: http://time.com/247/millennials-the-me-me-me-generation/

Suarez, J. G. (2016, Nov 24). *A baby boomer's guide to managing millennials at work*. Retrieved June 12, 2017 from Los Angeles Times: http://www.latimes.com/business/la-fi-career-coach-boomers-millennials-20161124-story.html

Sundar, S. S. (2008). "The MAIN Model: A Heuristic Approach to Understanding Technology Effects on Credibility". (M. Flanagin, J. Metzge, & A. J., Eds.) *Digital Media* , 73-100.

Sweeney, R. (2006). Millennial Behaviors & Demographics. 1-10. Newark, NJ.

The Keys to Unlocking the Millennial Mindset. (2016, Sept. 8). Retrieved June 13, 2017 from Nielsen.com: http://www.nielsen.com/us/en/insights/news/2016/keys-to-unlocking-the-millennial-mindset.html

Tilley, P. W. (2016, June). Nietzsche's Perspectivism in Truth and Narrative. 1-13. Sidney, Australia.

Tulgan, B. (2013). *Meet Generation Z: The second generation within the giant "Millennial" cohort*. Retrieved June 18, 2017 from Rainmaker Thinking: http://www.rainmakerthinking.com/assets/uploads/2013/10/Gen-Z-Whitepaper.pdf

Twenge, J. (2006). *Generation Me: Why Today's Young Americans are More Confident, Assertive, Entitled – and More Miserable than Ever Before*. New York: Free Press.

United States. (n.d.). Retrieved June 3, 2017 from Census Reporter: https://censusreporter.org/profiles/01000US-united-states/

What is Respect to a Millennial, a Boomer, and a Gen X'er? (2016, February 16). Retrieved August 29, 2017 from U.S. Chamber of Commerce Foundation: http://institute.uschamber.com/is-respect-different-for-millennials/

Williams, T. (n.d.). *Racial Diversity: There's More Work to be Done in the Workplace.* Retrieved jUNE 3, 2017 from The Economist: https://execed.economist.com/blog/industry-trends/racial-diversity-there%E2%80%99s-more-work-be-done-workplace

Wilson, M. a. (2008). How Generational Theory Can Improve Teaching: Strategies for Working with the "Millennials". *Curresnts in Teaching and Learnng, 1* (1), 29-44.

Zagenczyk, T. J. (2017). *The Moderating Effect of Psychological Contract Violation on the Relationship between Narcissism and Outcomes: An Application of Trait Activation Theory.* Retrieved July 22, 2017 from Frontiers in Psychology.

Chapter 5

DIGITAL NATIVES

W HOEVER DISCOVERED the wheel did not impress his/her family. Those Bronze Age Mesopotamian neighbors called it a waste of time, complained more effort should go into hunting, and worried what those living in the next hut would say.

So, the wheel was stored in the attic where it stayed until a grandchild found it and played with it. A nefarious neighbor, one of those who took the bite out of the apple, the one with more sticks and stones than anyone else, offered some sort of deal for the wheel with its plans, permits, and patents. The inventor's family never saw the neighbor again because he had moved west to what they called "Granite Valley." But, before they knew it, everyone in their part of the evolving world was moving on wheels.

Millennials were born into a similar warp in time, a time when no one understands where we are and where we are going. We may live during an age they have not labeled. Unnamed forces relieve and stress us. We may be approaching singularity.

Baby Boomers remember computers as punch card sorters and accelerated calculators. The personal computer entered the home as a gaming device. The internet was created for university use. And peripherals like the mouse, floppy discs, and more are beyond obsolete.

Millennials have been born into a culture still unable to grasp the digital effects on their work and personal lives. A sober reflection on what has happened in the past 25 years is staggering, but the average end-user cannot comprehend next steps in the digital age. But, Millennials are so much in sync with the current they take much for granted, find it fun, and work to master it.

Millennials speak digital. Their composition and reporting skills suffer, so they deem them less important and replaceable. But, the programming language they speak and work with says much about their worldview and character.

Programming is lateral. Because spoken and written languages are also ordered, the programming can arrange, sort, and search word and sentence order. Given that analogy, programmers forget that irony, innuendo, sarcasm, joy, passion, and more human expressions involve layers of meaning and usage most programming ignores.

They have a point. Anything not clear and flat lacks clarity and communication. But, this variance seems at odds with tradition and their elders' perception of things. If digital excludes the analog it also excludes metaphor. When coding, even the intellectually loaded concept of "if," "then," and "therefore" have only meaning in terms of calculation.

Millennials are, some more and some less, engineers by instinct. Engineers work in absolute confidence in outcomes. They work in heuristic confidence that solutions are reachable. Issues without problems interest them less, and the past even less. Thanks to the internet, they know everything or have access to all things known. Anything else does not engage.

WHAT IS A DIGITAL NATIVE?

A simple approach defines "digital native" as "an individual who was born after the widespread adoption of digital technology."[97] More relevant, Marc Prensky "defines digital natives as those born into an innate 'new culture' while the digital immigrants are old-world settlers, who have lived in the analogue age and immigrated to the digital world."[98] The long and short of this is that, when a Baby Boomer criticizes a younger cohort for not knowing how to dial a phone, the Boomer is at fault.

Prensky focuses on education. But, his analysis is relevant to the problem digital natives present the "digital immigrants." In "Digital Natives, Digital Immigrants," Marc Prensky writes,

As Digital Immigrants learn – like all immigrants, some better than others – to adapt to their environment, they always retain to some degree, their "accent," that is, their foot in the past. The 'digital immigrant accent' can be seen in such things as turning to the Internet second rather than first, or in reading the manual for a program rather than assuming that the program itself will teach us to use it. Today's older folk were 'socialized' differently from their kids."[99]

As nascent engineers, "Digital natives view the world horizontally, in equalitarian terms. Rather than dividing the world into hierarchies, they see everyone as existing on an equal level. They embrace the benefits of sharing things and ideas with each other and, in doing so, they cross boundaries. They are driven by values. Many of them are distrustful of traditional cultural and social institutions: marriage, religion, government. In opting out of these institutions, they have

---

97   (Digital Native, n.d.)

98   (Oliver, 2012)

99   (Prensky, 2001)

---

declared themselves microsegments of one — free agents."[100]

Millennials came into a world of change, as defined by the events of 9/11 terror and by the scenarios of Mortal Combat. Any discussion of when the web came into the picture or what they owe to their predecessors holds no interest. It is a done deal.

At the same time, they are pleased to be part and people of the new world, proud to be defining it, and eager to facilitate its next phase.

WORKPLACE ISSUES

As digital natives, Millennials differ from other generations. And, that presents problems for the workplace. Pew Research has listed several new "realities" that come with the generation of digital natives. The content is summarized here:

1. As video gamers, they have different expectations about how to learn, work, and pursue careers. "For companies, this puts a premium on designing engaging work that allows workers to make a clear contribution and be rewarded for same. If 'organization man' has become 'gaming man, then the importance of worker morale is elevated — as is the value of basing work on completed tasks, rather than other measures of work effort such as hours on the job."[101]

2. Being that it's not good enough to say, 'I read it on the internet,' without taking other steps to verify it."[102]

3. As "content creators," their notions of privacy and property differ from older generations. Every Millennial uses the internet to put their respective face on things, shape their identities, and create

---

100 (DeGraff, 2004)

101 (Rainie, 2006)

102 (Rainie, 2006)

images of themselves and their lives for sharing. For many users, this democracy of use also leads to shared gossip, misconceptions, bullying, and other problematic anti-socializing behaviors that employers can ill afford. It can also "justify" theft, compromise, and sharing of corporate intellectual property.

4. Product and people ranking informs and shapes their notions of propriety. This is the wisdom-of-the-crowd generation that has grown up rating athletes, women's appearances, movies, teachers, consumer products, restaurants, and more. "The tone of online commentary is often flame-oriented, racy, and retaliatory. This, too, is the generation that has given rise to cyberbullying."[103]

5. Multitaskers often live "in a state of 'continuous partial attention' that means the boundary between work and leisure is quite permeable."[104] Millennials multitask as a norm, but that also means moving quickly between work and chat, research and shopping, project management and entertainment. This means that "Those who operate in such a state are not as productive as those who stay on task."[105] This partial attention blurs different spheres of life and work allowing none of them a hierarchical importance. If "performance" means "getting the work done," how it gets done is less important to the worker.

These realities translate into challenges for the employer. Among the apparent negatives:

1. Millennials "need to be connected 24/7... This 'always-on' lifestyle is jam-packed with multitasking, defined by fast-paced communications, and increases workplace spontaneity with less concern about planning out the day."[106]

103 (Rainie, 2006)
104 (Rainie, 2006)
105 (Rainie, 2006)
106 (Hahn, 2015)

2. Millennials blur life and work. In doing so, they blur accountabilities. An addiction to socializing on phones and devices distract the worker.

3. Millennials can mistake processing volumes of information for work accomplished. When that frees them to work outside the office or at nomad locations, some control is lost.

4. Millennials communicate constantly but not always productively or appropriately. Their need to network and collaborate can be counterproductive.

5. Millennials confuse accessible information with quality information. They rarely differentiate quantity from quality.

"Given what we know about the characteristics of the digital workforce and the increasing use of technology at work, the question remains regarding how organizations can most effectively manage the digital workforce and leverage technology while avoiding potential downsides."[107]

LEVERAGE IS THE SOLUTION

Workers outside the Millennial generation, those digital immigrants, create management problems when they fail to embrace and integrate what values the digital natives bring to their production. As they insist on making Millennials work their legacy ways, the digital immigrants waste time, create resentment, and miss the point.

The point is that digital natives do not know any better, but that does not make them bad people or workers. Their numbers, interests, competencies, and skills mean all the difference in a competitive global economy. While the elders may have equity sweat in the business, the Millennials own it, so when management leverages their future, it is not surrendering. Rather, it is making a prudent and productive move.

---

107 (Colbert, Yee, & & Gerard, 2006)

» Leadership must see the value in letting Millennials have a true say in the design of work. They need more than token representation, and where their individual competencies warrant, they should lead design teams. "Research is needed to determine how to design jobs in ways that best leverage digital fluency and to explore how variance in digital fluency impacts conflict and collaboration in diverse groups."[108]

» Recruiting must focus on what soft skills digital natives bring to their presence. They need writing and spoken communication skills, social skills, and personal characteristics like patience, willingness, and respect for others. If the business is not prepared to teach these skills and their value, it should recruit what Netflix calls "fully-formed adults."

» Recruiting must take part in the leveraging by promoting the business's willingness to meet the digital natives on more than a level playing field. Recruiting advertising must present opportunities in a form and on platforms that digital natives find comfortable and attractive.

» Businesses must drop chalk and talk onboarding and training. An acculturation does not work when packaged in a 3-ring binder or PowerPoint presentation. Millennials seek engagement in gamification, and gamification can deliver any lessons on policy and procedure. It can also save money, time, and personnel distribution.

» Leadership must create a business architecture that develops mindfulness in its managers and employees. Millennials may need instruction on business practices, ethics, and propriety. They must understand the importance of privacy and intellectual property. But, leadership also must communicate those concerns in media and methods millennials find engaging. So, one way to assure this

108 (Colbert, Yee, & & Gerard, 2006)

connection is to bring Millennials into the conversation of priorities and method.

Peter Kasahara recommends the WASABI-formula[109], an acronym to help leadership optimize the presence and role of their digital natives:

> » **W**ork-Life Flexibility

The Millennials' ability to and addiction to blurring lines between work and life requires business leaders to create a corporate culture where flexibility is possible and promoted. Diverse workforces and compliance-bound Human Resources must support the flexibility that allows for leaves, creative experiences, related education, and the like.

> » **A**ccess to the Flow

Millennials do not expect participation; they mandate it. Led by Mihaly Csikszentmihalyi, positive psychologists Martin Seligman, Howard Gardner, and others have brought value to the concept of "flow." Flow is a point in real-time where people feel engaged and included in the growth and development of an organization.

Your digital natives know the flow of deep involvement in gaming, and they

> » **S**pace for Collaboration

Millennials find office cubicles hostile and claustrophobic. For them to perform, management must understand that collaboration is psychological, technological, and spatial. Since childhood, they have partnered with peers in Sunday School, scouts, and school. They expect to be heard and their voice respected.

They expect and need the best technology available. That starts with an individual perspective, so getting everyone on the same operational page is an IT challenge. Management must also give them the physical space that invites and enables cooperation and shared inputs.

---

109 (Kasahara, 2016)

» **A**ll-Generations Intelligence

Kasahara likes the phrase "All-Generations Intelligence"[14] to describe the potential that lies in the workplace with multiple generations. With the right architecture and culture, such organizations are positioned to optimize their diversity. Any such structure would require readjustment by senior workers and training younger hires in the soft skills so many find lacking.

» **B**usiness Strategy

Once your business has done what it can to engage its Millennials, it must "justify" the effort by aligning those efforts and outcomes with larger business strategies.

Such alignment will not happen without the active input of the digital natives expected to deliver. Leadership must invite, enable, and integrate their contributions in a culture of positive psychology and psychological safety. Allowing digital natives to design the work in this way also brands your business as an "employer-of-choice."

» **I**nspiration

Only leadership can make the preceding possible and practiced. It takes leadership to frame the proposition, to make it happen, and to inspire others to buy-in and follow. They once called this "walking the talk." But, this formula wants more than clichés. This is forward thinking and not past compliant.

WELCOMING MILLENNIAL WORKERS

Executive leadership must welcome and embrace its digital natives. It must create a climate they understand, and it must recognize that their respective talents change. For instance, the youngest of your Millennial digital natives

1. **Make them intrapreneurs**. Leadership's task lies in maintaining the balance an active and intrapreneurial workforce. It starts with catering to their need for freedom. They resist firm and unrelenting work schedules. They will continue to keep their social networking going.

   Again, you need to design the work with their input. If complying with a time-clock is no longer a metric for performance, you must ask the digital natives how they would rate the work in terms of timeliness, quality, and profitability. You want to seek their input on targets and coach them on the value of their elders' opinions.

2. **Give them ownership.** Micro-management stifles accountability and ownership. Digital natives would prefer the freedom to find means and solutions to clear objectives. They are all about the getting there.

   If you have created a psychologically safe environment, you also establish a trust. If leadership is authentic and transparent, digital natives will give up some of their self-interest. If you pay attention and personal credit to them, they will remain loyal.

3. **Reverse mentoring benefits all.** While Millennials have a generation's ego, they are still persons-in-the-making. They're not ready to admit that, but they welcome valuable input more than it may seem.

   If they can maintain their posture of equality, they appreciate mentoring from elders if it makes usable sense. Their mentors should coach gingerly by allowing the mentee to feel ownership and respect. But, reverse mentoring asks the new digital natives to coach their senior cohorts in skills unique to their experience.

   Leadership must blur any hierarchical lines in favor of formal and informal mentoring. This means assigning people to places and work where their digital skills are needed or where they might improve. Digital natives like sharing, but to some extent, it must be on their own terms.

The leadership and its culture must become transformational instead of incremental and transactional. "Digital transformation is not the destination, it's a journey – and your organisation's digital natives are ideally placed to become the guides. They can play a crucial role as influencers, supporting the digital immigrants as they adopt new ways of working, and creative ways of engaging with customers. They can help make sure the transformation journey brings the entire business along with it, not just the digitally-savvy few."[110]

4. **Reward immediately.** Digital natives are also an Amazon generation. They expect to get their delivery immediately. One solution is to keep them aligned with a career path, a picture that is in front of them every day. They do not value promises, but they value progress.

Millennials do not value gift cards, plaques, or watches. They respond better to voiced acknowledgment. This takes a cultural infrastructure where praise is immediate and specific to the work, person, and team. An increasing number of employers are using real-time software where managers and co-workers can comment on progress and people. And, more employers are doing away with traditional annual performance reviews.

Prompt and personal recognition feeds the Millennial passion for change, and change is positive and future-vested. Millennials see progress as horizontal, and emphasis on the hierarchical only thwarts their future. Hierarchies are not conducive to fluidity, flexibility, and freedom.

---

110 (Burke, 2017)

This also means making room for errors and failure. A growth organization budgets for fluctuation. It needs resilience and redefinition. It values fluidity and flow.

Businesses must concede that Millennials are digital natives. They must embrace all that means instead of encouraging a conflict dynamic. They must engage and expense these talents, leverage their skills, and recognize their performance.

You need a climate and organizational structure that allows digital natives to design their work, mentor upstream, and collaborate fully across operational functions. They are customers and creators. And, they can make or break your business future.

REFERENCES

Burke, T. (2017, July 11). Digital Natives or Digital Immigrants? 3 Tatics to Manage Multigenerational Digital Transformation. Retrieved August 18, 2017, from Atmosphere: http://www.weareatmosphere.com/digital-natives-3-tactics-multigenerational-digital-transformation/

Colbert, A., Yee, N., & & Gerard, G. (2006). The digital workforce and the workplace of the. Academy of Management Journal, 59(3), 731-739. Retrieved August 17, 2017, from http://ink.library.smu.edu.sg/cgi/viewcontent.cgi?article=6041&context=lkcsb_research

DeGraff, J. (2004, June 16). Digital Natives vs. Digital Immigrants. Retrieved August 16, 2017, from Huffington Post: http://www.huffingtonpost.com/jeff-degraff/digital-natives-vs-digita_b_5499606.html

Digital Native. (n.d.). Retrieved August 16, 2017, from TechPedia.com: https://www.techopedia.com/definition/28094/digital-native

Hahn, H. (2015, September 17). Digital Natives: They are changing the workplace culture. Retrieved August 11, 2017, from HR.com: https://www.hr.com/en/topleaders/all_articles/digital-natives-they-are-changing-the-workplace-cu_ienuu4w4.html

Kasahara, P. (2016, November 11). Dealing with digital natives: The wasabi-formula to spice-up your leadership style. Retrieved August 7, 2017, from Yale School of Management: http://som.yale.edu/blog/dealing-with-digital-natives-the-wasabi-formula-to-spice-up-your-leadership-style

Oliver, J. (2012, December 8). What does it mean to be a digital native? Retrieved August 16, 2017, from CNN: http://www.cnn.com/2012/12/04/business/digital-native-prensky/index.html

Prensky, M. (2001, October). Digital Natives, Digital Immigrants. On the Horizon, 9(5), 6. Retrieved August 16, 2017, from https://www.marcprensky.com/writing/Prensky%20-%20Digital%20Natives,%20Digital%20Immigrants%20-%20Part1.pdf

Rainie, L. (2006, September 28). New Workers, New Workplaces: Digital 'Natives' Invade the Workplace. Retrieved August 14, 2017, from Pew Research Center: http://www.pewinternet.org/2006/09/28/new-workers-new-workplaces-digital-natives-invade-the-workplace/

Chapter 6

NARCISSISM

PULITZER PRIZE WINNER, Louis "Studs" Terkel (May 16, 1912 – October 31, 2008) was the voice of the American worker. In at least one radio interview, he interviewed three generations of men involved in a family-owned car garage. Each of the men – the grandfather, son, and grandson – had a negative impression of his preceding generation.

While each agreed with the principle of customer service, each had a different spin on what the customer wanted and what he could bring to the need. For example, the son wanted to *renew* the car while his father wanted to *repair* it. Each thought he was right, but that does not make them narcissistic. Yet, Millennials must live down the accusation that their generation may be the most narcissistic of all time.

In his much quoted *The Culture of Narcissism*, Christopher Lasch wrote, "Every society reproduces its culture – its underlying assumptions, its modes of organising experience – in the individual, in the form of personality."[111] He wrote that the "celebrity culture, the radical movements of the 1960s and the dawn of the 'information age' had normalised a strain of selfishness that was once deemed pathological."[112]

Today's Millennial critics are quick to repeat Lasch's assertions. And,

---

111 (Maughan)
112 (Maughan)

I agree with his assumption that "every society reproduces its culture." But, there are real problems with his description of a generation manifesting "a strain of selfishness that was once deemed pathological." After all, Lasch made these claims in 1979. So, whom was he writing about? The Millennials of 1979 or 2017?

Like so many other generalizations, it speaks of a non-differentiated generation, a naive assumption. For example, the cell phones that enabled selfies and chatting weren't introduced until 2007 and may mark a change in basic assumptions for the generation he was describing in 1979.

Millennials have shown a different social behavior. Their sense of self, its value, and their role differs from the traditional. The specific signs and causes deserve analysis. But, the analysis should belie any claim the generation has elevated selfishness to a pathological level. Management must understand this "narcissism" for what it is and learn to harness its values.

Millennials' predecessors

"Some psychologists suggest increased narcissism in society has resulted in increased aggression and self-promotion and reduced empathy and pro-social behaviors, and is potentially even responsible for the perceived 'bad behavior' of the Millennial generation."[113]

Psychologists make a distinction between "normal" and "pathological" narcissism.

> » "Normal" narcissism is associated with increased self-image and a "go-get-em" attitude."
>
> » "Pathological" narcissists ignore the feelings and wishes of others and expect to be treated as superior, regardless of their actual status or achievements.

---

113 (Zagzencyk)

"How do we distinguish healthy self⊠interest from pathological narcissism, usually referred to as narcissistic personality disorder?"[114] "To be diagnosed as a 'pathological narcissist' medically by a psychiatrist, a person's behavior must deviate significantly from what is expected, and it must cause significant personal or interpersonal problems across situations, and not be due to drugs, medications, or medical conditions."[115]

But, "Narcissism is a pervasive, endemic aspect of contemporary life, and exists to varying degrees in each and every one of us. We all need some measure of healthy narcissism to get on in the world, which is related to self-esteem, confidence, sense of significance, etc. And most of us suffer to some extent from some pathological or neurotic narcissism as well."[116]

"They're young and full of themselves, like every other generation that's come before them was at some point."[117] But, are they more narcissistic than The Greatest Generation? The Baby Boomers spawned criminal financial leaders like Enron's Kenneth Lay and Andres Fastow, Countrywide's Angelo Mozilo, Bear Stearns' Fabrice "Fabulous Fab" Tourre, Lehman Brothers CEO Richard Fuld, Bear Stearns CEO Jimmy Cayne, Merrill Lynch CEO Stan O'Neal, CEO of Merrill Lynch, Citigroup CEO Chuck Prince. Scandals at Bernie L. Madoff Investment Securities, Washington Mutual, AIG, Bayou Hedge Fund, Adelphia Communications, WorldCom, Lincoln Savings & Loan, and more were all in the hands of Baby Boomers.

"Boomers blew through resources, racked up debt, and brought an end to economic growth, using their enormous voting power to elect politicians who enacted policies that typically benefitted Boomers' interests, rather than future generations. Now, Millennials face more debt, fewer resources and higher levels of unemployment than their

114 (Gabard)
115 (Are Millennials Really Narcissists?)
116 (Diamond)
117 (Foster)

parents, and are likely to see the fallout of runaway environmental destruction within their lifetimes."[118]

But, it's also true that Boomers effected the Civil Rights Era, served honorably in Viet Nam, died in the 9/11 tragedies, and created most of the revolutionary changes in medicine, technology, and the arts. Boomers include Barack Obama, Oprah Winfrey, Deepak Chopra, Bill Gates, Bruce Springsteen, Tony Blair, Peter Frampton, Kareem Abdul-Jabbar, Steve Jobs, and tens of thousands of other worthy influencers.

Millennials enjoy the legacy of the best of the Boomers. However, they are closer in time to the financial and political bad choices of Boomers since the Clinton administration. As they matured, they lost faith in the entrenched institutions of Congress, Wall Street, mainstream media, organized religion, and much more.

Their experience has proven a great leveler. Millennials feel equal to-often superior to-those who authored their present situation. And, that galls their seniors.

IT'S IN THE NUMBERS

Millennials admit they are more narcissistic than preceding generations. Of 750 surveyed, "Millennials ages 18 to 25 rate themselves at 61.4 on a zero-to-100 scale of narcissism. They ranked adults 60 years and up as 38 on the same scale, a 23-point difference."[119] At the same time, their elders find the difference much bigger; "60 years and older ranked Millennials at 65.3 on the 100-point narcissism scale, and ranked themselves at a mere 26.5, a spread of nearly 40 points."[120] The disparity reflects on the small survey sample, but it suggests that each generation goes through the same perception.

118 (Gregoire)
119 (Pappas)
120 (Pappas)

Joshua Grubbs at Case Western Reserve University conducted experiments that found:

» "In the last decade, popular writings have portrayed Millennials as exceptionally self-centered, creating a prevailing narrative that has become accepted as fact, to a degree, due to its repetition."[121]

» "Millennials experience more anger, frustration and sadness over the label than other generations... Even if they agree with it to some extent, it still bothers them."[122]

» "What may seem like signs of 'narcissism' or self-obsession to one person may be evidence of 'individualism -- a trait valued by millennials—to someone else."[123]

» As further "proof," Jean Twenge's research conclusions are quoted here:[124]

» Millennials are less likely than Boomers or Gen-Xers to say they are concerned about social problems, interested in politics and government, to contact public officials or to work for a political campaign.

» Millennials are less likely to trust the government to do what is right, and less likely to say they are interested in government and current events.

» Millennials are less likely to say they do things to conserve energy and help the environment. They are also less likely to agree that government should act on environmental issues.

» Millennials are also less likely to say they want a job helpful to others or worthwhile to society.

---

121 (Millennials admit to being narcissists, but don't you dare call them that)
122 (Millennials admit to being narcissists, but don't you dare call them that)
123 (Millennials admit to being narcissists, but don't you dare call them that)
124 (Eckman)

This counters earlier assumptions (as in Howe and Strauss's book) about Millennials expressing concern for others and desiring to volunteer their time and efforts to help others.

She cites Christian Smith's position: "The idea that today's emerging adults are as a generation leading a new wave of renewed civic-mindedness and political involvement is sheer fiction. The fact that anyone ever believed that idea simply tells us how flimsy the empirical evidence that so many journalistic media stories are based upon is and how unaccountable to empirical reality high-profile journalism can be."[125]

However, the Twenge data has spawned considerable criticism that her numbers follow from flimsy and unreliable data and poor research methodology. For instance, a study at the University of Illinois concluded, "This leads to the obvious conclusion that finding young people to be narcissistic is an aging phenomenon, not a historical phenomenon. The fact that one can find complaints about the younger generation being more narcissistic going back to Hesiod helps make the point that every generation is Generation Me. That is, until they grow up."[126]

The conclusion follows research on two issues:

1. When new data on narcissism is folded into pre-existing meta-analytic data, there is no increase in narcissism in college students over the last few decades.

2. Age changes in narcissism are both replicable and large compared to generational changes in narcissism.

They quote the ancient Hesiod (700 B.C.), "I see no hope for the future of our people if they are dependent on the frivolous youth of today, for certainly all youth are reckless beyond words. When I was a boy, we were taught to be discrete and respectful of elders, but the

---

125 (Eckman)
126 (Roberts, Edmonds and Grijalva)

present youth are exceedingly wise and impatient of restraint."[127] "Every generation is Generation Me, as every generation of younger people are [sic] more narcissistic than their elders."[128]

IT'S A VOCABULARY PROBLEM

The American Psychiatric Association defines "narcissism" as "a pattern of need for admiration and lack of empathy for others. A person with narcissistic personality disorder may have a grandiose sense of self-importance, a sense of entitlement, take advantage of others or lack empathy."[129]

The APA identifies narcissistic behaviors, behaviors published in Diagnostic and Statistical Manual of Mental Disorders (DSM–5). The DSM lists the following diagnostic symptoms of Narcissistic Personality Disorder (NPD):[130]

1. Expects to be recognized as superior without commensurate achievements

2. Preoccupied with fantasies of unlimited success, power, brilliance, beauty, or ideal love

3. Believes s/he is "special" and unique and can only be understood by, or should associate with, other special or high-status people (or institutions).

4. Requires excessive admiration

5. Possesses sense of entitlement, i.e., unreasonable expectations of especially favorable treatment or automatic compliance with his/her expectations

---

127 (Roberts, Edmonds and Grijalva)
128 (Roberts, Edmonds and Grijalva)
129 (What are Personality Disorders?)
130 (Diagnostic criteria for 301.81 Narcissistic Personality Disorder)

6. Takes advantage of others to achieve his/her own ends

7. Lacks empathy, unwilling to recognize or identify with the feelings and needs of others

8. Envies of others or believes that others are envious of him/her

9. Shows arrogant, haughty behaviors or attitudes

You should notice the weighted criteria are subject to some subjective evaluation: *grandiose, preoccupied, special, excessive, unreasonable, exploitative, unwilling, envious,* and *arrogant.* Such terms reduce the effectiveness of diagnostic metrics.

If you rate these behaviors on a scale, any combination of scores can be counterproductive or productive. For instance, the NPD may also drive ambitious, confident, and self-interested people to success and leadership positions. Psychiatric practitioners in the 1930's labeled a "healthy narcissism" to describe "normal, even desirable, aspects of being in the world: general well-being, self-assurance, self-assertion, satisfaction with who one was."[131]

When it comes to Millennials, the critics use "narcissist" in the pejorative sense. It makes them unlikeable and pathologically disagreeable. But, the fact is that we generally "find narcissists more likeable, attractive, and exciting than non-narcissists, and that we are drawn to their "sexy" charisma and confidence. In addition, narcissists can succeed in corporate settings, as long as they stay on narcissism's healthy side. Boards want self-confident, assertive, and creative leaders—all traits fueled by healthy narcissism. The trick is to stay on the healthy side, to not give into the grandiosity and recklessness that can go with pathological narcissism."[132]

Ambition, confidence, forthrightness, independence, and optimism do not make Millennials pathologically narcissistic or counterproductive.

131 (Lumbeck)

132 (Lumbeck)

Sure, there are losers in the class, but that should not tar the entire generation.

DON'T ROCK THE BOAT

Many of the problems with the Millennials' alleged narcissism lie in the perception by their elders in the workplace. Those Boomers belonged to a very homogenized generation. Boomers are highly structured in their socioeconomic zeitgeist. They keep their hands in the boat, and they resist rocking it. They believe in athletic teams, military might, and organized religion as living forces. That leaves them fearing individualism.

Boomers have been collectivists. They value the group more than its individuals. The group acts collectively, and its individual members share and respect its group values. Boomers consider themselves as Americans, Republicans, Jews, professionals, laborers, and such. It also identifies them as reactionaries, racists, and vigilantes.

Existentialism and its contemporary paradigm shifts gave individuals a more active and articulate role. As collective influences weakened or collapsed, individual liberty and self-reliance have grown influentially. The rebellion against collectivist restraints arose in the 1960's in movements against war, racism, and social inequities.

The movement increased the value of human reason and individual conscience. This new democracy insists that the individual has the right to selfishness-even if it is not an inherently admirable trait. Millennials, if they act collectively, find themselves entitled and enabled to define themselves as individuals.

So, to the extent they align with history at all, they are transcendentalists, pantheists, and followers of Thoreau. They enjoy their self-determined "alienation" as a badge of honor, value, and virtue.

Self-reliant, self-aware, self-conscious, they resent implications that they are egotists, selfish, and self-centered. The Kardashians are not role models for the most or best of them.

Extreme narcissistic behaviors can disturb the work process and the workers' environment.

» **Know-It-Alls** offer unsolicited opinions on whatever topic comes up. Absent a ready topic, they put their opinion forward as authoritative. They disdain or disturb collaboration, lecture more than listen.

» **Self-Important** colleagues blow their own horns, loudly and constantly. Such people believe themselves exceptional and destined to higher desserts. If charismatic, their attractiveness is shallow and short-lived.

» **Manipulators** seek support and recognition through flattery and seduction. They gossip, and use and abuse people in their efforts to advance. They will trade alliances and friendships to move forward casting aside colleagues with indifference.

» **Bullies** humiliate those around them in small and big ways. They are mean, distasteful, and often brutal in word and action. They are contemptuous, insidious, and threatening. But, they often go unnoticed because of their victims' fears or management's indifference.

» **Destructive narcissists** do not seek to coexist. They seek to kill anything and anyone in their way. They will lie about you, sabotage your work, and poison the well in which you work.

Disruptive narcissists should be dealt with promptly and authoritatively. If corrective action will change the behavior, you might give it a chance when the circumstances permit. Identifying toxic narcissists and dealing with them does not happen in a vacuum. Any effective discipline must comply with common and related laws.

Recognition, correction, and resolution cannot interfere with product or conflict with corporate goals. But, some habits can help redirect alleged narcissists in the workplace:

» Understand the Narcissistic Personality Disorder is not personal.

» Ignore the problem because it will likely move on if it evokes no response.

» Give them credit publicly where it makes sense and is deserved.

» Disagree clearly and unequivocally before you explain why, but don't make it personal.

» Keep eye contact.

» Avoid empathy or talk of feelings because it means little to them.

» Insist that you are offended or insulted when it applies.

» Learn what matters to the person and acknowledge it.

You must remember that narcissists are not aware of their NPD as a deep-seated problem in low self-esteem and vulnerability. Everything just seems less valuable or unimportant to them. But, lest disorder become normal in the workplace dominated by Millennials, you can develop defenses:

» Writing trumps speaking in this world. If you commit narcissists to putting plans or suggestions in writing, you press them to deliver. If you have them share the ideas in writing before discussion, everyone comes to the table with the same materials. The narcissist idea, thereby, becomes a common effort.

» Partner one narcissist with another. Their mutual competitiveness and individual egotism drives them to produce a better single outcome.

» Exploit your narcissists. If they appear as charismatic and charming on the surface, you can assign them to self-centered and high-energy roles in sales pitches, training presentations, and public appearances.

But, what happens when your boss is a narcissistic Millennial? With the broad definition of Millennials and their huge presence in the workplace, the narcissist in your life may be your boss. These suggestions owe a great deal to suggestions and phrasing by Rebecca Knight:[133]

» **Know what you are dealing with.** Bosses invariably have a certain dynamic personality. They can be dynamic, personable, and charismatic without being narcissistically self-centered. Chances are they are confident, experienced, and outspoken. But, that doesn't make them bad.

What makes them "bad" is a question of degree. If they make dynamism boorish, personality offensive, and charism annoying, you may have a problem.

» **Maintain your own self-esteem.** Pathological narcissists feed on your character. They target your self-esteem with demeaning and stressful experiences. You can balance the insult with activities outside work that give you pleasure and build your self-worth. Spending time with your family, taking part in a sport, or volunteering for community work will help your morale independent of your work life.

» **Flatter the egotist.** You can manage the narcissist by flattering him/her. If it feels bad or makes you uncomfortable, don't do it. But, you can return the boss the same kind of insincere praise because flattery will get you everywhere with a narcissist.

You can certainly be neutral, diplomatic, or non-committal. It's to your credit to give the boss credit where deserved. If you can focus on the boss's strengths, you can support and advocate his/her interests. If you find this is living a lie, you need not compromise your character. But,

133 (Knight)

if salvaging the boss's talents is important to you and the business, you will find a way to compromise.

> » **Return the favor.** If your boss has earned the position rightfully or has been promoted for his/her talents or potential, there must be something you can profit from. Narcissists have energy, communication skills, high energy, visionary strategy, and more.

With some objective analysis, you can emulate the best and least objectionable of their behaviors. You can parse their performance and adopt their better selves. The worst thing you can do is to criticize the boss. That is playing the narcissist's game. But, you can help the boss succeed, help them shape a best practice, or help them prepare what it is in their own best interest.

> » **Avoid watercooler gossip.** Sabotage and subterfuge are the narcissist's forte. They are tough to beat at their own game. The worst of them verge on the paranoiac, ready to see enemies everywhere and eliminate them at all costs.

You can vent to your spouse and family—if not on social media. Any reputable organization will have someone in the role of an ombudsperson to listen actively to your concerns as valued feedback. As a trusted third party, they can assess the validity and impact of your input.

> » **To quit or not to quit.** You will find an advantage in giving this time. If the narcissistic presence is too strong, it will take a toll on you physically and emotionally. But, if you allow it time, you can control your own position.

Leaving the job may be your best and smartest option, but you want to leave on your own terms. You should bide your time, hone your resume, and start your job search. If in other ways you find the work imaginative, creative, engaging, and satisfying, you need to find a way to stay until the narcissist loses value.

YOUR MANAGEMENT STRATEGY

As a manager of Millennials, you have a challenge. It should begin with an understanding that Millennials are not more narcissistic than their elders. Many of them may be behind their chronological age in terms of social acclimation, but they are not pathologically narcissistic.

If you understand that, you will have a better perspective on how you can optimize their energy, dynamic, and charisma. Your organization needs every strength they bring as individuals.

This may mean a top down readjustment in management and Human Resources practices. It may mean recruiting best matches to your culture or presenting your culture as an employer of choice to fully formed adults. And, it may mean profile testing to differentiate the toxic narcissist from the powers you need to compete.

Chapter 7

MILLENNIALS AND INSTITUTIONS

MILLENNIALS BELONG to a class of people far more democratized than previous generations. Social hierarchies have collapsed on their own or proven ineffective and irrelevant. Forces of immigration and intermarriage have diluted their homogenous origins. And, they have profited from increased diversity and gender balancing so much that, for most of them, differences go unnoticed.

They do defer to those who win their games, but such deferral does not equal abject obedience. For them, collaboration defines their social, political, and economic coexistence. With everyone equal, only institutions stand in the way of fraternity and egalitarianism.

Every age has taken selfies with whatever technology it had at hand. So, this desire to self-express does not equal self-absorption. They believe their generation has the power–and unique dedication–to change the world through collective power. "From school uniforms to team learning to community service, Millennials are gravitating toward group activity." [134]

Contradicting the assumption of their narcissism and self-absorption, they have created a new sense of family. Heirs to a divorce culture, Millennials look for means and measures to strengthen and support the

---

134 (Howe)

---

institution of marriage. And, they find it in multigenerational living and other group settings.

The social, economic, and technological context that has informed Millennials has also designed them, altered their cellular structure, so to speak. Context has shaped their values and valuation processes. For instance, as divorce increased, children raised in single parent environments learned to distrust and measure hierarchies differently. They try to balance the subsequent insecurity with their individual ability to handle the insecurity. If they do not regress and internalize fears, their healthiest option is self-awareness and self-confidence.

No longer pressed to marry early, they apparently take longer to mature. In fact, they can prolong their self-development, self-discovery, and self-expression. The development also helps them discover and value empathy for issues larger than themselves. So, the same people accused of being self-interested and selfish find and run charity marathons, work well in collaborative teams, and contribute more than they own.

RESPECTING INSTITUTIONS IN THEIR OWN WAY

Classic institutions have failed Millennials. As we said earlier, this generation has no sense of or need to belong. Those groupings have failed them repeatedly, but they understand the need for form and infrastructure.

As the fake news continues to describe them as disrespectful and narcissistic, we would like to do some fact checking here:

» According to a 2016 Gallup report, of the 73 million Millennials counted, "59% of Millennials are single and have never been married and 60% of Millennials do not have any children under 18 in their household."[135]

---

135 (Fleming)

While they are in no hurry to marry, they are intent on having children. Women are choosing when to have children, and they are increasingly waiting for the life-work balance they expect from quality employers.

Gallup also reports, "59% of Millennials are single and have never been married, and 60% of Millennials do not have any children under 18 in their household."[136]

This waiting is much their choice. But, it also affects their maturing process as it forestalls the responsibility and accountability that accompany parenthood. For employers, this means having to accommodate the parental leave of experienced talent.

> » According to Pew Research, "The number and share of Americans living in multigenerational family households has continued to rise, even though the Great Recession is now in the rear-view mirror. In 2014, a record 60.6 million people, or 19% of the U.S. population, lived with multiple generations under one roof."[137]

Multigenerational family living—defined as households that include two or more adult generations, or one that includes grandparents and grandchildren—is growing among nearly all U.S. racial groups as well as Hispanics, among all age groups and among both men and women. "The share of the population living in this type of household declined from 21% in 1950 to a low of 12% in 1980. Since then, multigenerational living has rebounded, increasing sharply during and immediately after the Great Recession of 2007-09."[138]

"In 2009, 51.5 million Americans (17% of the population) lived in multigenerational households, according to data from the Census Bureau's American Community Survey. In 2012, 57 million Americans – 18% of the U.S. population – were part of multigenerational homes,

---

136 (Fleming)

137 (Cohn)

138 (Cohn)

---

according to the last major Pew Research Center analysis of this data."[139]

Millennial men feel "'doing good' is increasingly connected to creating greater balance and harmony between work and family. They have become more egalitarian in relationships, including at work, and are less likely to think of themselves as the sole breadwinner, not surprisingly."[140] This keeps them in multi-generational, domestic partnerships, and group living environments where tasks and accountabilities are collegial.

There are many positives in these family arrangements. They show respect for legacy and tradition. But, the pattern also impacts their sense of independence and self-reliance, virtues the Great Generation claims to own.

» They are the children of a divorced generation, the Baby Boomers. "The U.S. has the highest divorce rate in the Western world. The data show clearly that the longer we wait to get married the more successful our marriages will be. And it's not like we can't move in together in the meantime: the rate of unmarried cohabitation has risen 1,000% over the past four decades."[141]

This suggests Millennials wait to marry for complex reasons, some of which are self-serving. Jessica Bennett quips, "For a generation reared on technology, overwhelmed by choice, feedback and constant FOMO [fear of missing out], isn't testing a marriage, like we test a username, simply ... well, logical?"[142]

Millennials do not disrespect the institution of marriage, but they want to manage it on their terms. They are more inclined to marry across color, religious, and income lines. Women are more likely to initiate a marriage, and couples are more likely to cohabit for several years before the marriage.

---

139 (Cohn)
140 (Anderson)
141 (Bennett)
142 (Bennett)

"About 70 percent of marriages that begun in the 1990s reached their 15th anniversary...up from about 5 percent of those that began in the 1970s and 1980s. Those who married in the 2000s are so far divorcing at even lower rates. If current trends continue, nearly two-thirds of marriages will never involve divorce."[143]

> » • According to Pamela Paxton, "sociologists have theorized that people who feel vulnerable or disadvantaged for whatever reason find it riskier to trust because they're less well-fortified to deal with the consequences of misplaced trust."

Older people simply do not feel the loss Millennials experienced during The Great Recession. Even though it did not measure up to The Great Depression, it is central to their experience. They suffered from their parents' losses and their own, perhaps more aware of the happenings than earlier generations thanks to the internet. It has put them in debt and as wary of financial institutions and big business as the Boomers.

> » The events of 9/11 remain at the center of the Millennials' experience. They have witnessed atrocities and genocide committed in the name of religion. And, they have seen traditional religious organizations unwilling or unable to run interference, let alone able to address social inequities and global suffering.

Thanks to scandals like the clerical sexual abuse of children, they have moved from traditional institutions in droves. However, consistent with their generation's ethos, "they are more likely to have a 'do-it-yourself' attitude toward religion."[144]

Research shows that fewer Millennials are affiliated with any specific formal faith. "Young adults also attend religious services less often than older Americans today. And compared with their elders today, fewer

---

143 (Miller)
144 **Invalid source specified.**

young people say that religion is very important in their lives."[145]

Their church attendance is less frequent than their ancestors, but like them, it increases with age. Studies indicate, "Less than half of adults under age 30 say that religion is very important in their lives (45%), compared with roughly six-in-ten adults 30 and older (54% among those ages 30-49, 59% among those ages 50-64 and 69% among those ages 65 and older). By this measure, young people exhibit lower levels of religious intensity than their elders do today, and this holds true within a variety of religious groups."[146]

Millennials do feel they are the arbiters of what is "authentic," and they find both institutional rituals and trendy ceremonies inauthentic. Self-disclosed responses to a survey by Bama Group found, "among young people [with a Christian experience] who don't go to church, 87 percent say they see Christians as judgmental, and 85 percent see them as hypocritical."[147]

Results also show, "67 percent of Millennials prefer a 'classic' church over a 'trendy' one, and 77 percent would choose a 'sanctuary' over an 'auditorium'."[148] Less than 50% believe in God, but that does no discourage their interest in prayer or meditation. What they say is most attractive is a quiet sanctuary, and the only communities of faith that attract them must be inclusive.

At the same time, each week, 20- to 40-thousand Millennials attend mega-churches like Rick Warren's purpose-driven Saddleback Church, Joel Osteen's prosperity preaching Lakewood Church, and Chris Hodges' Church of the Highlands. They may be attracted to the non-denominational status, the diverse and active social ministries, and the teaching that God shows his pleasure with material prosperity. This

145 **Invalid source specified.**
146 **Invalid source specified.**
147 **Invalid source specified.**
148 **Invalid source specified.**

seems to contradict their distaste for institutions, but the membership tilts to the older Millennials with families.

» Millennials have served in the military for more than 16 years of war. One Boomer writes, "Millennials question authority more than generations of the past, and texting and engaging on social media comes naturally, but no one should doubt that this generation is any less patriotic than previous ones. The heroic stories of self-sacrifice by this generation on the battlefield and the endearing sense of optimism by those Millennials wounded in recent wars are humbling."[149]

Cotford and Sugarman looked at the Millennials and their attitudes toward the military. And, they notice several characteristics:

» This generation is broadly unfamiliar with the military, its culture, its basic structure, and its function.

» Millennials do not exhibit the same open antagonism towards service members felt during the Vietnam era, yet neither do many of them understand the difference between a sailor, a soldier, an airman, and a Marine.

» They understand that the military is hierarchical but may not be able to explain the difference between a second lieutenant and a lieutenant colonel.

» They may not appreciate how much autonomy and responsibility an enlisted "grunt" may have had while deployed to an Afghan village, or how little influence even a high-ranking officer may have had in planning the war in Iraq.

Without understanding the basics of military structure and culture, Millennials are liable to underappreciate the positive contributions of some service members, misattribute blame for failures to others, and,

---

149 (Aldrich)

---

overall, fundamentally misconceive the nature of the military and its relationship with civilian policymakers and civil society.

At the same time, the military has processed millions of Millennials into society and the workplace. "As the country has become more racially and ethnically diverse, so has the U.S. military. Racial and ethnic minority groups made up 40% of Defense Department active-duty military in 2015, up from 25% in 1990. (In 2015, 44% of all Americans ages 18 to 44 were racial or ethnic minorities.)"[150] They enter with a diversity experience, emotional maturity, and leadership potential that others lack.

» According the Harvard University School of Politics, fully 88 percent of Millennials say they only "sometimes" or "never" trust the press.[151] Millennials see political leaders as failures, polity as ineffective. Millennials are finding more engaging public service options.

As *The Atlantic* says, "It's easy to throw Millennials and their 'incoherent' politics under the bus—especially when they believe the government should be doing a better job... [but while accusations] have branded Millennials as a politically indifferent and disconnected generation, their reputation betrays an emerging and distinct identity of civic activism."[152]

Huffington Post summarized findings of a Case Foundation "Millennial Impact Report:"[153]

» Millennials are most interested in education, healthcare, and the economy.

» They identify as more conservative-leaning than liberal, but those claiming conservative orientation are moderate to liberal conservatives.

---

150 (Parket)

151 (Cilliza)

152 (When It Comes to Politics, Do Millennials Care About Anything?)

153 (Ryan)

» 54% see themselves as activists.

» Most Millennials believe they can have an impact on the country.

» More than half trust the government "only a little or not at all." 44 percent trust it "some or a lot."

» When it comes to supporting community projects affiliated with causes they care about, Millennial support rose to 56%.

» 36% of Millennials get involved in demonstrations such as rallies, protests, boycotts, and marches.

» Nearly two-thirds of Millennials post on social media at least once per week. Conservative-leaning Millennials use social media to post about and/or engage with issues they're most interested in more than liberals.

» From March to May of 2016, Millennials who indicated they would either not vote for any of the candidates or would not vote at all both increased.

Millennials do not trust the Presidency, Supreme Court, Congress, Wall Street, mainstream news media, banks, or the medical system. Only local police, military, and colleges and universities get positive votes.

BUSINESS TO MILLENNIALS

The evidence shows Millennials do not appreciate our current institutions. But, that's not to say they reject institutions. You must remember that Boomers wouldn't trust anyone over 30—until they turned 30.

They have the numbers, power, and inclination to do well in this world. But, technology and other forces have divorced them from the past. Confident in their ability and hugely optimistic about their ability to change things, the past has no intellectual or practical importance.

The past is obsolete, past upgrading or refurbishing.

Among their numbers sits a growing underclass of educated people who cannot find employment appropriate to their history. It includes those who are underemployed and underpaid. But, it also includes large numbers of those who have just given up finding futures they were taught to expect. We see many of these attracted to alt-right and alt-left politics. Angry, frustrated, and alienated, they can make difficult and belligerent employees.

Millennials clearly choose options unknown to or unimportant to their seniors. And, they have low tolerance for anything structural that gets in the way of their achieving goals now.

» Millennials are not a homogenous group. They generally have no specific regional, ethnic, religious, or political bias. For one key thing, they vary significantly in age. The youngest of them varies greatly in personality and values from the older members. This asks managers to improve their own flexibility, adaptivity, and re-silience.

» They expect to be heard. So, the challenge to management is to make that easier. But, they also expect their feedback to be used, integrated, or explained away.

» Millennials do not need managers to be friends. They want appre-ciation for the work. So, managers do better to move away from personnel performance appraisals on the person towards assess-ing the quality of the task completed.

» Their sense of teamwork differs from that co-opted from Japanese quality initiatives. Perhaps because they owe so much to multi-generational living, their idea of collaboration is more collegial. Where collaboration needs pitching in, collegiality emphasizes a shared responsibility.

» Millennials have little interest in hierarchical distinctions like job titles. One way they read that is that they have rights to what they need. Managers would lead by providing purpose and all the information necessary to achieve success in individual tasks and career paths.

» They will repeatedly ask "why not?" And, management should realize the question is not provocative or disrespectful. It seeks only to identify and remove the barriers to getting things done.

» That Millennials move from job to job reflects as much on the economy and the nature of global competition as it does from disloyalty. Nonetheless, management must step up to manage talent issues where they will find that loyalty is earned and tested on the work floor. If employees are being lured away by competitors, management must look at what it can do better and not at the character of Millennials.

Businesses that have transparent commitment to purpose build institutions that command the loyalty and commitment of their Millennial employees. They must want to work with you to achieve something of value.

REFERENCES

21 Strengths Arising From Military Experience. (n.d.). Retrieved June 3, 2017 from University of Vermont: https://www.uvm.edu/~career/pdf/21_Strengths_Arising_From_Military_Experience_61670_7-1.pdf

(2016). *50 Best Workplaces for Diversity.* Fortune.

Age and Sex Composition: 2010 Census Briefs. (2011, May). Retrieved June 3, 2017 from census.gov: https://www.census.gov/prod/cen2010/briefs/c2010br-03.pdf

Aldrich, J. (2016, October 11). *Military Millennials: A Boomer's perspective.* Retrieved October 1, 2017 from Military1: https://www.military1.com/military-lifestyle/article/1643297014-military-millennials-a-boomers-perspective/

Allen, N. J. (1990). The measurement and antecedents of affective, continuance and normative commitment to the organization. *Journal of Occupational and Organizational Psychology , 63* (1), 1-18.

Allen, R., Allen, D., Karl, K., & White, C. (2015). Are Millennials Really an Entitled Generation? An Investigation into. *Jounral of Business Diversity , 15* (2), 14-26.

Anderson, K. (2013, October 5). *Baby Bust: Millennials' View Of Family, Work, Friendship And Doing Well.* Retrieved September 11, 2017 from Forbes: https://www.forbes.com/sites/kareanderson/2013/10/05/baby-bust-millennials-view-of-family-work-friendship-and-doing-well/#28bea6b02af0

Are Millennials Really Narcissists? (2016, July 31). Retrieved July 22, 2017 from neuroamer.com: https://neuroamer.com/2016/07/31/are-millennials-really-narcissists-lets-look-at-data/

Ashgar, R. (2014, Jan 13). *What Millennials Want In The Workplace (And Why You Should Start Giving It To Them).* Retrieved May 16, 2017 from Forbes: https://www.forbes.com/sites/robasghar/2014/01/13/what-millennials-want-in-the-workplace-and-why-you-should-start-giving-it-to-them/#a95c7014c404

Aubrey, L. C. (2012, March 15). The Effect of Toxic Leadership. Carlisle, PA, USA: United States War College.

(2016). *Bank of America/USA TODAY Better Money Habits® Report: Young Americans & Money*. Bank of America/USA Today.

Bennett, J. (2014, July 04). *The Beta Marriage: How Millennials Approach 'I Do'*. Retrieved October 1, 2017 from Time: http://time.com/3024606/millennials-marriage-sex-relationships-hook-ups/

Berry, B. (2015, February 15). *An Interview with John Pendergast*. Retrieved April 10, 2017 from Conscious Variety: http://www.consciousvariety.com/articles/john-prendergast

Biggert, N. (1977). The Creative-Destructive Process of Organizational Change: The Case of the Post Office. *Administrative Science Quarterly , 22* (3), 16.

Bowman, J. (2015, May 14). *The Secret to PepsiCo, Inc.'s Success*. Retrieved January 13, 2017 from fool.com: http://www.fool.com/investing/general/2015/05/14/the-secret-to-pepsico-incs-success.aspx

Bruneau, M. (2016, May 26). *7 Behaviors of successful entrepreneurs*. Retrieved June 18, 2016 from Forbes: http://www.forbes.com/sites/meganbruneau/2016/05/26/7-things-successful-entrepreneurs-do/#3a112991625b

Calvin, G. (2012, June 11). *Indra Nooyi's Pepsi challenge*. Retrieved January 13, 2017 from Hingam Schools.com: http://hpswebs.hinghamschools.com/hhs/teachers/sgeorge/pepsi%20article.pdf

Calvin, G. (2016, Oct 21). *Three Big Mistakes Leaders Make When Managing Millennials*. Retrieved June 14, 2017 from Fortune: http://fortune.com/2016/10/21/millennials-workplace-management/

Cilliza, C. (2015, Apr 30). *Millennials don't trust anyone. That's a big deal.* Retrieved May 16, 2017 from The Washington Post: https://www.washingtonpost.com/news/the-fix/wp/2015/04/30/millennials-dont-trust-anyone-what-else-is-new/?utm_term=.a2453525bffc

Cohn, D. a. (2016, August 11). *A record 60.6 million Americans live in multigenerational households.* Retrieved September 30, 2017 from Pew Research Center: https://www.pewresearch.org/fact-tank/2016/08/11/a-record-60-6-million-americans-live-in-multigenerational-households/

Confidence in Institutions. (2016, June 5). Retrieved June 12, 2017 from Gallup.com: http://www.gallup.com/poll/1597/confidence-institutions.aspx

(2017). *Corporate Equality Index 2017: Rating Workplaces on Lesbian, Gay, Bisexual and Transgender Equality.* Washington, D.C: Human Rigths Campaign Foundation.

Cotford, M. a. (2016, August 2). *Millennials And The Military.* Retrieved September 25, 2017 from Hoover Institute: http://www.hoover.org/research/millennials-and-military

Dizikes, P. (2014, Oct 7). *Study: Workplace diversity can help the bottom line.* Retrieved June 4, 2017 from MIT News: http://news.mit.edu/2014/workplace-diversity-can-help-bottom-line-1007

Dziuban, C., Moskal, P., & Hartman, J. (n.d.). Higher Education, Blended Learning and the Generations: Knowledge is Power No More.

Employment Situation of Veterans — 2016. (2017, March 22). Retrieved June 3, 2017 from Bureau of Labor Statistics: https://www.bls.gov/news.release/pdf/vet.pdf

Espinoza, C., & Uklelja. (2016). *Managing the Millennials: Discover the Core Competencies for Managing Today's Workforce* (2nd ed.). Hoboken, NJ: John Wiley & Sons.

Feeman, M. (2016). Rewriting the Self: History, memory, narrative. New York, New York, USA: Rutledge. Retrieved April 10, 2017 from https://books.google.com/books?hl=en&lr=&id=97tmCgAAQBAJ&oi=fnd&pg=PP1&dq=describe+the+human+condition+against+our+historical+memory&ots=3yNJT9qZ4z&sig=aqtcQlActVGRltpSmG--3Uafk47E#v=onepage&q&f=false

Fleming, J. (2014, May 19). *Gallup Analysis: Millennials, Marriage and Family.* Retrieved September 30, 2017 from Gallup News: http://news.gallup.com/poll/191462/gallup-analysis-millennials-marriage-family.aspx

Flood, A. (2015). *The female millennial: a new era of talent.* PWC.

Fry, R. (2016, April 25). *Millennials overtake Baby Boomers as America's largest generation.* Retrieved June 3, 2017 from Pre Research: http://www.pewresearch.org/fact-tank/2016/04/25/millennials-overtake-baby-boomers/

Gabbard, G. O.H. (2016). The many faces of narcissism. *World Psychiatry, 15* (2), 115-116.

Generational Breakdown: Info About All of the Generations. (n.d.). Retrieved June 3, 2017 from The Center for Generational Kinetics: http://genhq.com/faq-info-about-generations/

Generational Differences Chart. (n.d.). WMFC.org.

Gierenzer, G., & Gaissmaier, W. (2011). Heuristic Decision Making. *Annual Review of Psychology* , 451-481.

Gilbert, J. (2011, Sept/Oct). *The Millennials: A new generation of employees, a new set of engagement policies.* Retrieved June 3, 2017 from Ivey Business Journal: http://iveybusinessjournal.com/publication/the-millennials-a-new-generation-of-employees-a-new-set-of-engagement-policies/

Goldsmith. M. and Carter, L. (Ed.). (2010). *Best Practices in Talent Management: How.* San Francisco, CA, U.S.A.: John Wiley & Sons, Inc.

Green, A. (2015, February 2). *5 Ways Employers Discourage You From Negotiating Salary.* Retrieved May 16, 2016 from U.S. News Money: http://money.usnews.com/money/blogs/outside-voices-careers/2015/02/02/5-ways-employers-discourage-you-from-negotiating-salary

Harris, T. (1993, May-June). The Post-Capitalist Executive: An interview with Peter F. Drucker. *Harvard Business Review* .

Hebert, J. (26, Jan 2017). *Why Millennials Deserve More Respect at Work.* Retrieved May 13, 2017 from Fortune: http://fortune.com/2017/01/26/millennials-2/

Hofstrand, D. (2010, February). *Peter Drucker and Innovation.* From Iowa State University Extension and Outreach: http://www.extension.iastate.edu/agdm/wholefarm/html/c5-10.html

Howe, N. a. (2000). *Millenials are Rising: The Next Great Generation.* New York: Vintage.

Howe, N., & Nadler, R. (2010, Aug 25). *Managing Millennials: How to Cope With a Generation of Multitaskers.* Retrieved June 20, 2017 from eremedi.com: https://www.eremedia.com/tlnt/managing-millennials-how-to-cope-with-a-generation-of-multitaskers/

Howe, N., & Strauss, W. (1991). *Generations: The History of America's Future, 1584 to 2069.* New York: William Morrow & Company.

Howe, N., & Strauss, W. (2007, July-August). The Next 20 Years: How Customer and Workforce Attitudes Will. *Harvard Business Review* , 13.

Hudson, B. T. (1994, June). *Innovation through Acquistion.* Retrieved January 13, 2017 from The Cornell H.R.A. Quarterly: http://journals.sagepub.com/doi/pdf/10.1177/001088049403500318

Hunt, V. L. (2015, Jan). *Why diversity matters.* Retrieved June 3, 2017 from McKinsey & Company: http://www.mckinsey.com/business-functions/organization/our-insights/why-diversity-matters

"Pro-business," but expecting more: The Deloitte Millennial Survey 2017. (2017, May 13). From Deloitte: https://www2.deloitte.com/global/en/pages/about-deloitte/articles/millennial-survey-pro-business-but-expecting-more.html

Jenkins, R. (2017, August 7). *Why Millennials Are So Entitled (Parents Are Partly Blamed).* Retrieved August 29, 2017 from Inc.: https://www.inc.com/ryan-jenkins/this-is-why-millennials-are-entitled.html

Kaneshige, T. (2013, Oct 10). *Why Managers Need to Stop Worrying and Love Millennials.* Retrieved May 13, 2017 from CIO: http://www.cio.com/article/2381827/leadership-management/why-managers-need-to-stop-worrying-and-love-millennials.html

Kiisel, T. (2012, May 16). *Gimme, Gimme, Gimme -- Millennials in the Workplace.* Retrieved June 18, 2017 from Forbes: https://www.forbes.com/sites/tykiisel/2012/05/16/gimme-gimme-gimme-millennials-in-the-workplace/#738daed1bcea

Kraus, L. (2017). *2016 Disability Statistics Annual.* University of New Hampshire. Durham, NH: Institute on Disability/UCED.

Kriegel, J. (2015, May 29). *Why Generational Theory Makes No Sense.* Retrieved June 14, 2017 from Forbes.com: https://www.forbes.com/sites/oracle/2015/09/29/why-generational-theory-makes-no-sense/#156566678eaa

Lee Badgett, M., & others. (2013). *The Business Impact of LGBT-Supportive Workplace Policies.* Los Angeles: The Williams Institute.

Lizardo, O. (2004). The Cognitive Origins of Bourdieu's Habitus. *Journal for the Theory of Social Behaviour 34:4 , 34* (4), 375-401.

McCord, P. (2014, Jan-Feb). *How Netflix Reinvented HR*. Retrieved June 21, 2017 from Harvard Business Review: https://hbr.org/2014/01/how-netflix-reinvented-hr

Meyer, K. (2016, Jan 3). *Millennials as Digital Natives: Myths and Realities*. Retrieved May 14, 2017 from Neilsen Norman Group: https://www.nngroup.com/articles/millennials-digital-natives/

(2011). *Millennials at work: Reshaping the Workplace*. PWC.com.

Millennials in Adulthood: Detached from Institutions, Networked with Friends. (2014, March 7). Retrieved June 3, 2017 from Pew Research Center: http://www.pewsocialtrends.org/2014/03/07/millennials-in-adulthood/

Millennials: Confident. Connected. Open to Change. (2010, Feb 24). Retrieved May 13, 2017 from Pew Rsearch Center: Millennials: Confident. Connected. Open to Change

Miller, C. C. (2014, December 2). *The Divorce is Over, but the Myth Lives On*. Retrieved October 1, 2017 from The New York Times: The Upshot: https://www.nytimes.com/2014/12/02/upshot/the-divorce-surge-is-over-but-the-myth-lives-on.html

Modaity. (n.d.). Retrieved June 12, 2017 from https://multimodalityglossary.wordpress.com/multimodality/

New Times for Multimodality? Confronting the Accountability Culture. (2012, May). *Journal of Adolescent & Adult Literacy* , 8.

Nuwer, R. (2014, April 8). *Andy Warhol Probably Never Said His Celebrated "Fifteen Minutes of Fame" Line*. Retrieved June 11, 2017 from Smithsonian Magazine: http://www.smithsonianmag.com/smart-news/andy-warhol-probably-never-said-his-celebrated-fame-line-180950456/

Onion, R. (2015, May 15). *Against generations*. Retrieved June 14, 2017 from AEON.com: https://aeon.co/essays/generational-labels-are-lazy-useless-and-just-plain-wrong

Pappas, S. (2016, Feb 8). *Why Are Millennials Narcissistic? Blame Income Inequality.* Retrieved July 20, 2017 from LiveScience.com: https://www.livescience.com/53635-why-millennials-are-narcissistic.html

Parket, K. C. (2017, April 13). *6 facts about the U.S. military and its changing demographics.* Retrieved October 1, 2017 from Pew Research C enter: https://www.pewresearch.org/fact-tank/2017/04/13/6-facts-about-the-u-s-military-and-its-changing-demographics/

Patten, E., & Fry, R. (2015). *How Millennials today compare with their grandparents 50 years ago.* Pew Research Center.

PepsiCo Earnings Preview: Snacks Could Offset Decline In Beverage Sales. (2014, February 11). Retrieved January 16, 2017 from Forbes: http://www.forbes.com/sites/greatspeculations/2014/02/11/pepsico-earnings-preview-snacks-could-offset-decline-in-beverage-sales/#7acac6e12d65

PepsiCo. (2016). *PepsiCo Reports Third Quarter 2016 Results.* PepsiCo.

Perna, M. (2016, Mar 5). *Millennials & Respect: Why It Matters So Much.* Retrieved May 16, 2017 from Linkedin: https://www.linkedin.com/pulse/millennials-respect-why-matters-so-much-mark-perna

Pisker, L. (2017, Jan 18). *Challenging Modern Society: Disabled Millennials.* Retrieved June 3, 2017 from Yout Time Magazine: http://www.youth-time.eu/articles-opinions/challenging-modern-society-disabled-millennials

Ponteriero, C. (2016, June 17). *11 institutions trusted more by millennials.* Retrieved June 12, 2017 from Property and Casuality 360°: http://www.propertycasualty360.com/2016/06/17/11-institutions-trusted-more-by-millennials

Rebell, R. (2016, Oct 10). *RPT-COLUMN-For millennials, adulthood now defined by financial freedom.* Retrieved July 22, 2017 from Reuters.com: http://www.reuters.com/article/column-money-adulthood-repeat-column-per-idUSL1N1CG1AS?type=companyNews

Ryan, S. (2017, July 1). *New Report: Millennials' Political Behavior Will Surprise You.* Retrieved September 28, 2017 from Huffington Post: http://www.huffingtonpost.com/ryan-scott/new-report-millennials-po_b_10764426.html

Sasse, B. (2017). *The vanishing American Adult: Our Coming of Age Crisis - and How to Rebuid a Culture of Self-Reliance.* New York: St. Martin;s Press.

Stein, J. (2013, May 20). *MIllennials: The Me Me Me Generation.* Retrieved July 22, 2017 from Time.com: http://time.com/247/millennials-the-me-me-me-generation/

Suarez, J. G. (2016, Nov 24). *A baby boomer's guide to managing millennials at work.* Retrieved June 12, 2017 from Los Angeles Times: http://www.latimes.com/business/la-fi-career-coach-boomers-millennials-20161124-story.html

Sundar, S. S. (2008). "The MAIN Model: A Heuristic Approach to Understanding Technology Effects on Credibility". (M. Flanagin, J. Metzge, & A. J., Eds.) *Digital Media* , 73-100.

Sweeney, R. (2006). Millennial Behaviors & Demographics. 1-10. Newark, NJ.

The Keys to Unlocking the Millennial Mindset. (2016, Sept. 8). Retrieved June 13, 2017 from Nielsen.com: http://www.nielsen.com/us/en/insights/news/2016/keys-to-unlocking-the-millennial-mindset.html

Tilley, P. W. (2016, June). Nietzsche's Perspectivism in Truth and Narrative. 1-13. Sidney, Australia.

Tulgan, B. (2013). *Meet Generation Z: The second generation within the giant "Millennial" cohort.* Retrieved June 18, 2017 from Rainmaker Thinking: http://www.rainmakerthinking.com/assets/uploads/2013/10/Gen-Z-Whitepaper.pdf

Twenge, J. (2006). *Generation Me: Why Today's Young Americans are More Confident, Assertive, Entitled – and More Miserable than Ever Before.* New York: Free Press.

United States. (n.d.). Retrieved June 3, 2017 from Census Reporter: https://censusreporter.org/profiles/01000US-united-states/

What is Respect to a Millennial, a Boomer, and a Gen X'er? (2016, February 16). Retrieved August 29, 2017 from U.S. Chamber of Commerce Foundation: http://institute.uschamber.com/is-respect-different-for-millennials/

When It Comes to Politics, Do Millennials Care About Anything? (n.d.). Retrieved September 22, 2017 from The Atlantic: http://www.theatlantic.com/sponsored/allstate/when-it-comes-to-politics-do-millennials-care-about-anything/255/

Williams, T. (n.d.). *Racial Diversity: There's More Work to be Done in the Workplace.* Retrieved jUNE 3, 2017 from The Economist: https://execed.economist.com/blog/industry-trends/racial-diversity-there%E2%80%99s-more-work-be-done-workplace

Wilson, M. a. (2008). How Generational Theory Can Improve Teaching: Strategies for Working with the "Millennials". *Curresnts in Teaching and Learnng, 1* (1), 29-44.

Zagenczyk, T. J. (2017). *The Moderating Effect of Psychological Contract Violation on the Relationship between Narcissism and Outcomes: An Application of Trait Activation Theory.* Retrieved July 22, 2017 from Frontiers in Psychology.

Chapter 8

BUILDING COLLABORATION

EVEN MILLENNIALS do not know what "collaboration" means. The word has been thrown around, co-opted, misused, and dulled by ubiquitous repetition. Some would be surprised that "collaboration" once meant a traitorous connection with the enemy.

With the rise of Japanese quality initiatives, it became synonymous with teamwork. But, the whole concept needs some reconsideration considering the importance Millennials place on collaboration.

Collaboration is a tactic, a means to achieve purpose. A company that values collaborative outcomes is one that creates and sustains an environment that facilitates employee collaboration. But, that's not explanation enough.

SYNCHRONOUS COLLABORATION

As with so many things, "synchronous collaboration" is a tech term. It refers to audio and video chatting among all participants in real time. Members use phones, Skype, and meeting platforms to put it together.

The immediacy of the contact facilitates sharing of information and problem solving. At best, it speeds up process by pulling together key personnel at one time if not in one place. The dynamic created by a real-time event energizes interaction and innovation.

Synchronous collaboration improves the clarity in dealing with complex assignments. The speed reduces inefficiencies, and the interpersonal input eliminates redundancies. It communicates the context of tone, stress, and anxiety in which the project takes on dimension. And, this keeps the contributions aligned with corporate goals.

THE CLOUD

The cloud enables asynchronous collaboration. Any number of apps lets participants contribute at well or in their respective "real time." It encourages participants to drop notes or codes to spaces available to authorized parties. Sharable Google docs and Dropbox are simple versions of accessible, convenient, and scalable apps.

Asynchronous collaboration invites input from time zones throughout the world. It encourages contributions in the form of videos and slide presentations. It allows submission of prepared contributions and larger amounts of data.

This form of collaboration makes customers of participants letting them review and feedback at will. And, it presents material worth study, appreciation, and analysis; it encourages response that has taken advantage of the time exposed.

MILLENNIALS AND COLLABORATION

How the Japanese quality initiatives on collaboration moved into popular cultural behavior is a mystery. But, Millennials grew up with collaborative expectations. From Sunday school through soccer play, middle school, and college situations, they look forward to collaborative situations.

Educators, for example, develop curricula built on collaborative work in STEM courses. If diverse opinion brings value, students form study groups on their own or accept direction on problem solving. The generation has experience in having a say in scouts, school, and social behaviors.

Donna Kalikow, executive director of the Center for Public Leadership at Harvard University's Kennedy School of Government, describes the best version of this generation as "entrepreneurial, independent, tech savvy, tolerant and socially conscious... steeped in 'collaboration, cultural tolerance, conflict resolution, communication and 'followership' — the empowerment of colleagues who support a leader's vision'."[154]

You might appreciate the definition of "collaboration" published by the American Psychological Association. (Phrases are emboldened for emphasis.). "Collaboration is a **group problem-solving process** that **requires the creative integration of needs** and **joint ownership of decisions**. It involves working in teams, **coalitions**, alliances, partnerships, and networks. It involves **trust and consensus building**. It allows **different leadership styles to contribute simultaneously**. The **goal of collaboration** is not to **solve problems through** compromise but to achieve **synergies that lead to innovative solutions**."

Psychology Today cautions, "Collaborating involves substantial organizational commitment, a very high level of trust, and extensive sharing of turf. The qualitative difference between Cooperating and Collaborating is that collaborating partners demonstrate a public enthusiasm for—and commitment to the value of—learning from each other to become better at what they do collectively."[155]

That's an important distinction:

> » Collaboration differs from "networking" because networking is transactional, an exchange of data or information for mutual benefit.

154 (Goodheart)
155 (Mashek)

» "Coordination" expects cooperation from participants to, for instance, meet at the same time or develop a common agenda.

» "Cooperation" shares information and resources for mutual self-interest and to serve a common goal.

Millennials "have always been able to open multiple tabs in an Internet browser to conduct research... They are tech-savvy multi-taskers because that is all they have ever known. They don't view managers as content experts (like their predecessors) because they know where to find multiple versions of the information."[156]

Millennials find connectivity in collaboration. Exploiting the tools that make it happen comforts them. One study says, 39% of employees don't feel people in their organization collaborate enough. And, three out of four consider collaboration as "very important."[157]

Other research surveyed co-workers who, "When asked about the frequency of their collaboration with colleagues, partners, or vendors, almost all connected employees (98%) collaborate at some level. Nearly two thirds (65%) collaborate multiple times a day while only 2% stated that they never collaborate with others."[158]

The same report notes, "Millennials are the first generation to grow up in a connected world. And most do not remember a time without the Internet. They opt for quick, casual, and efficient collaboration and choose tools that meet these needs. Nearly half of Millennials (45%) said chatting or texting is their preferred way to collaborate with co-workers, vendors, or partners. Similarly, 47% of Millennials also favored online meetings to in-person if they were given the choice."[159]

---

156 (Brack)

157 (Infographic - Communicating in the Modern Workplace)

158 (Collaboration Trends and Technology: A Survey of Knowledge Workers)

159 (Collaboration Trends and Technology: A Survey of Knowledge Workers)

THE SHORTFALL OF INDIVIDUAL OWNERSHIP

Contributors to Harvard Business Review raise some common concerns: "Teamwork all too often feels inefficient (search and coordination costs eat up time), risky (can I trust others to deliver for my client?), low value (our own area of expertise always seems most critical), and political (a sneaky way of self-promoting to other areas of one's firm). Lurking behind these reservations may be concerns about losing relevance, becoming one of those 'charismatic' leaders so often criticized as all form, no substance'."[160]

They recommend also understanding what collaboration is not (summarized here for brevity):

» **Collaboration is not a style**. It is not a leadership style in which relationships take precedence over the task at hand.

» **Collaboration is not consensus.** There must be clarity about where the buck stops.

» **Collaboration is not "cross-selling."** It rather requires working across organizational or disciplinary silos to holistically tackle sophisticated problems.

» **Collaboration is not always the answer.** Suitable for certain task, it is unsuitable for others and should not lead to endless meetings and struggles for consensus.

"Excess collaboration saps energy and leaves employees with too little time to complete their work during the day, forcing too many workers to spend time playing catch-up after hours and on weekends."[161]

And, here is the paradox presented when collaboration is not constructively managed. "In most cases, 20% to 35% of value-added collaborations come from only 3% to 5% of employees. As people

---

160 (Gardner)
161 (Mankins)

become known for being both capable and willing to help, they are drawn into projects and roles of growing importance. Their giving mindset and desire to help others quickly enhances their performance and reputation."[162]

This creates a risk of overloading that 3 to 5 percent of employees and creating bottlenecks to progress. But, the fears only prompt use to notch up our approach. Millennials somehow know this work better than their predecessors, so you need their help in formation.

This is not something learned or picked up late in the game. Active and successful participation is a talent worth recruiting. But, if you are the leader you need the experience to value the time, personnel, and resource issues.

CREATING COLLABORATIVE ENVIRONMENTS

It's clear that Millennials want and expect to work in collaborative environments. Still, we still do not have clarity on this. Ideally, collaboration is a shared work and accountability, and that takes more than connectivity. Collaboration is not committee work.

You have all participated in poorly run telephone or Skype meetings. In as many cases as not, participants find themselves in a barely listening, non-participatory role. There are many more group and team events that fail to produce or satisfy that Millennial need.

In a large sense, what you call "collaboration" is a transactional format. Participants pitch in prescribed amounts of work and skills. In the classic study group, portions of assignments are distributed, and individuals bring their completed segments back for group consumption. Some work can be divided up the same way.

---

162 (Cross)

In another sense, groups approach a project problem, and members contribute data and input on problem-solving approaches. This, too, is shared work. Contributions are proportionate with individuals recognized for their respective input.

Certain different tasks may benefit from different approaches, but the collaboration Millennials want and expect is something else. Millennials seek collaboration because it is psychologically self-confirming and because they value the collegiality when it works.

"Collegiality" means more than pitching in with a helping hand. It means sharing power and authority among your colleagues. Here are 10 tips on satisfying the Millennials in your workplace with engaging collaboration:

1. **Know yourself:** Collegiality calls for self-awareness. Self-aware-ness differs from self-perception or self-esteem. It requires you to assess your strengths and needs-to-improve regarding specif-ic projects. It helps you determine what you can contribute and what you need to learn.

2. **Respect others:** It's fair to assume that, if you were indeed the go-to-expert on the project, that you would not be on a team. Collegiality mandates that you value all contributions. Howev-er, this respect does not come intuitively. People are inclined to want credit when things go well and shift blame when things go wrong. Keeping participation transparent takes leadership effort and guidance.

3. **Mix it up:** Throwing teams together because they are in the same department or location works for some minor tasks like settling on a venue for the holiday party or scheduling the company soft-ball season. But, when you want to create innovation or solve problems, teams need selective diversity, talent variety, and per-formance records. Members must like challenges, be willing to speak up, and possess skills specific to the problem.

4. **Make it inter-disciplinary:** Diversity brings varied views, skills, and styles to the group. But, members must come to the group trusting that they can achieve goals—together. Members should understand that there is no need for the group if any individual has the solution in hand. Achieving this cross-disciplinary commitment and behavior requires members and managers to eliminate preconceptions and personal profiles.

   Some form of connectivity comes naturally. Negative people, for instance, always seem to form a clique around the watercooler or break room. Department members have functionality in common. Others will align along interests in college football, child rearing, or dozens of other common concerns. But, such clusters do not make for collegial collaboration.

   Productive and creative collaboration takes leadership and management. Management cannot casually name collaborators and walk away from their performance. Management must create and sustain a culture of collaboration.

5. **Create social opportunity:** Employees get to know each other at company picnics, community volunteer events, and the local pub. But, you want and need different sorts of social interaction to build the trust it takes to collaborate.

   One way to do this is to use open floorplans that invite gathering in conversation pits and free access to necessary resources. With no cubicles, no offices, no physical restrictions, barriers disappear circumstantially.

   The same physical layout might include sheltered spaces where workers can retreat or pursue their own work. Companies with the revenue also supply socializing spaces in childcare centers, restful gardens, or fitness centers.

Anticipating difficulty with distant participants who do not know their colleagues first hand, management should "pre-socialize" them. Managers can introduce them with content and visuals, even arrange early Skype connections.

6. **Choose the best and brightest:** Many workers get along comfortably with their peers. Many are likable and popular. But, that's not enough to make them a first choice.

Millennials are characteristically eager and addicted to connectivity. They seek reassurance and self-confirmation from leaders and fellows. But, their inclination to volunteer does not, on its own, make them collaborative players.

Instead, management must select individuals particularly strong in the problem subject area and who have demonstrated collaborative skills in the past. In addition, managers must structure the group and its process to include a few people who are new to the process or who need corrective action on collaboration behaviors.

Millennials may be "confident, self-expressive, liberal, upbeat and open to change." But, all Millennials are not these things or strong in these things. So, managements must recruit such talent. It needs the means to profile and test recruits for their fit.

7. **Discuss desired behaviors:** The business does not need groups that approach collaboration as if it were a tailgate meeting. Showing up on time does not serve the purpose of collaboration.

Video conferencing can draw together faces and voices from multiple distant locations or even people in a sprawling facility. The visual connection eliminates the social loafers, those who attend meetings without interest or involvement.

Management must provide clear objectives and metrics for completion and achievement (which are not necessarily the same thing). The objectives must clearly align with corporate goals, and standards of collaborative behavior must be drawn and discussed.

When possible, collaborative teams must exchange word of their respective skills and abilities in meetings structured to prepare for what management means by collaboration. Managers need demonstrated buy-in, willingness, and commitment.

8. **Require leaders to model collaborative behavior:** Effective collaboration only works when it is top down. Collaboration does not belong to one function or another. It does not belong at one level of the hierarchy or in one functional silo. It must be part of the culture, and that only happens when the leadership models the behavior and makes collaboration part of the business's vision and goals.

9. **Optimize technology:** Collaborative teams need the best tools available. They need the capital and resources to facilitate the collaboration and the process. And, they need the technology that makes it easier.

Millennials value the technology that assures their connectivity and real-time experience. They want to share at any hour from any place. and they want a common place where they can leave their contribution and forums where they can chat on materials.

They look for engagement with leader boards, dashboards, and visual representation of the work and its progress. And, they want the ability to enter feedback and receive recognition for their input.

Millennials look for the ability to collaborate on the move, from home, and at work wherever ideas strike them. And, this requires cloud-based resources usable across various systems, platforms, and devices.

10.**Measure what matters**: Making collaboration work challenges any compensation strategy. The most productive compensation programs will:

   » Reward customer service more than internal compliance.

   » Promote revenue generation instead of cost savings.

   » Emphasize productivity more than compliance.

   » Manage people not financial targets.

   » Implement 360° input and feedback technology.

It's a challenge to recognize and reward the A-players and still maintain the group dynamic. You can offer team rewards for meeting or exceeding team objectives. But, you risk losing the attention of star players. So, make the team award some bonding experience like additional vacation days or a group dinner.

Cash rewards in the form of bonuses or pay increases encourage resentment and negative internal competition. They may even prompt internal sabotage. So, it helps to keep groups small and well selected.

Solid management will model peer-to-peer communication and encouragement. Managers must lead communication that regularly revisits purpose, plan, and process. They must discuss and encourage dialog on accountability, individual and group roles, and the values of feedback and diverse views.

Smart mangers will "bargain" with group members to organize the team's purpose, goals, and functions. Allowing the members to select their leaders and assign accountabilities increases their buy-in.

What you want to measure and, therefore, reward are individual contributions to team outcomes. You want to reward their collaborative contributions, not their individual work or efforts. You want to reward the quality not the quantity of collaborative performance.

This takes work. "Haphazard development of diverse teams without provisions for training and conflict resolution mechanisms may end in unproductive and inefficient use of resources."[163]

To avoid this, management and members must understand, "greater value is created at all levels of analysis, micro, meso, and macro, as collaboration moves from sole creation to co-creation of value."[164] There is circular payback here. How well participants behave in this structured collaborative depends on how well they understand and value the co-creation of value. "Furthermore, there is a need to demonstrate how and to what extent social and environmental value creates economic value and vice versa, whether simultaneously or sequentially."[165]

Millennials appreciate this wisdom of the crowd more than they know, and while it may run counter to their elders' emphasis on individuality and self-reliance, it is producing undeniable benefits.

"Collaboration is the fuel of any business... a driving force for continued efficiency among everyday tasks and a necessity for improving the outcomes of many business activities."[166]

All work must be co-creative if it is to compete, and constructive collaboration remains the means to make that happen and to attract, retain, and sustain Millennials.

"Collaboration in the digital age can help spur original thinking with connections happening across locations and departments that couldn't have previously occurred. By nature, collaboration brings different voices, teams, specialties and opinions together to solve an existing problem or develop something completely new."[167]

---

163 (Jehn 24)
164 (Austin 929)
165 (Austin 960)
166 (Honigman)
167 (Honigman)

REFERENCES

21 Strengths Arising From Military Experience. (n.d.). Retrieved June 3, 2017 from University of Vermont: https://www.uvm.edu/~career/pdf/21_Strengths_Arising_From_Military_Experience_61670_7-1.pdf

(2016). *50 Best Workplaces for Diversity.* Fortune.

Age and Sex Composition: 2010 Census Briefs. (2011, May). Retrieved June 3, 2017 from census.gov: https://www.census.gov/prod/cen2010/briefs/c2010br-03.pdf

Aldrich, J. (2016, October 11). *Military Millennials: A Boomer's perspective.* Retrieved October 1, 2017 from Military1: https://www.military1.com/military-lifestyle/article/1643297014-military-millennials-a-boomers-perspective/

Allen, N. J. (1990). The measurement and antecedents of affective, continuance and normative commitment to the organization. *Journal of Occupational and Organizational Psychology , 63* (1), 1-18.

Allen, R., Allen, D., Karl, K., & White, C. (2015). Are Millennials Really an Entitled Generation? An Investigation into. *Jounral of Business Diversity , 15* (2), 14-26.

Anderson, K. (2013, October 5). *Baby Bust: Millennials' View Of Family, Work, Friendship And Doing Well.* Retrieved September 11, 2017 from Forbes: https://www.forbes.com/sites/kareanderson/2013/10/05/baby-bust-millennials-view-of-family-work-friendship-and-doing-well/#28bea6b02af0

Are Millennials Really Narcissists? (2016, July 31). Retrieved July 22, 2017 from neuroamer.com: https://neuroamer.com/2016/07/31/are-millennials-really-narcissists-lets-look-at-data/

Ashgar, R. (2014, Jan 13). *What Millennials Want In The Workplace (And Why You Should Start Giving It To Them).* Retrieved May 16, 2017

from Forbes: https://www.forbes.com/sites/robasghar/2014/01/13/
what-millennials-want-in-the-workplace-and-why-you-should-
start-giving-it-to-them/#a95c7014c404

Aubrey, L. C. (2012, March 15). The Effect of Toxic Leadership. Carlisle,
PA, USA: United States War College.

Austin, J. E. (2012, September 13). Collaborative Value Creation: A Review of Partnering Between Nonprofits and Businesses. Part 2: Part-
nership Processes and Outcomes. *Nonprofit and Voluntary Sector
Quarterly* , pp. 929-968.

(2016). *Bank of America/USA TODAY Better Money Habits® Report:
Young Americans & Money.* Bank of America/USA Today.

Bennett, J. (2014, July 04). *The Beta Marriage: How Millennials Approach 'I Do'.* Retrieved October 1, 2017 from Time: http://time.
com/3024606/millennials-marriage-sex-relationships-hook-ups/

Berry, B. (2015, February 15). *An Interview with John Pendergast.* Retrieved April 10, 2017 from Conscious Variety: http://www.con-
sciousvariety.com/articles/john-prendergast

Biggert, N. (1977). The Creative-Destructive Process of Organizational
Change: The Case of the Post Office. *Administrative Science Quarterly*
, *22* (3), 16.

Bowman, J. (2015, May 14). *The Secret to PepsiCo, Inc.'s Success.* Retrieved January 13, 2017 from fool.com: http://www.fool.com/invest-
ing/general/2015/05/14/the-secret-to-pepsico-incs-success.aspx

Brack, J. (2012). *Maximizing Millennials in the Workplace.* UNC-Kenan
Flagler Business School.

Bruneau, M. (2016, May 26). *7 Behaviors of successful entrepreneurs.*
Retrieved June 18, 2016 from Forbes: http://www.forbes.com/
sites/meganbruneau/2016/05/26/7-things-successful-entrepre-
neurs-do/#3a112991625b

Calvin, G. (2012, June 11). *Indra Nooyi's Pepsi challenge*. Retrieved January 13, 2017 from Hingam Schools.com: http://hpswebs.hingham-schools.com/hhs/teachers/sgeorge/pepsi%20article.pdf

Calvin, G. (2016, Oct 21). *Three Big Mistakes Leaders Make When Managing Millennials*. Retrieved June 14, 2017 from Fortune: http://fortune.com/2016/10/21/millennials-workplace-management/

Cilliza, C. (2015, Apr 30). *Millennials don't trust anyone. That's a big deal*. Retrieved May 16, 2017 from The Washington Post: https://www.washingtonpost.com/news/the-fix/wp/2015/04/30/millennials-dont-trust-anyone-what-else-is-new/?utm_term=.a2453525bffc

Cohn, D. a. (2016, August 11). *A record 60.6 million Americans live in multigenerational households*. Retrieved September 30, 2017 from Pew Research Center: https://www.pewresearch.org/fact-tank/2016/08/11/a-record-60-6-million-americans-live-in-multigenerational-households/

(2015). *Collaboration Trends and Technology: A Survey of Knowledge Workers*. Dimensional Research.

Confidence in Institutions. (2016, June 5). Retrieved June 12, 2017 from Gallup.com: http://www.gallup.com/poll/1597/confidence-institutions.aspx

(2017). *Corporate Equality Index 2017: Rating Workplaces on Lesbian, Gay, Bisexual and Transgender Equality*. Washington, D.C: Human Rigths Campaign Foundation.

Cotford, M. a. (2016, August 2). *Millennials And The Military*. Retrieved September 25, 2017 from Hoover Institute: http://www.hoover.org/research/millennials-and-military

Cross, R. R. (2016, January-February). *Collaborative Overload*. Retrieved September 24, 2017 from Harvard Business Review: https://hbr.org/2016/01/collaborative-overload

Dizikes, P. (2014, Oct 7). *Study: Workplace diversity can help the bottom line.* Retrieved June 4, 2017 from MIT News: http://news.mit.edu/2014/workplace-diversity-can-help-bottom-line-1007

Dziuban, C., Moskal, P., & Hartman, J. (n.d.). Higher Education, Blended Learning and the Generations: Knowledge is Power No More.

Employment Situation of Veterans — 2016. (2017, March 22). Retrieved June 3, 2017 from Bureau of Labor Statistics: https://www.bls.gov/news.release/pdf/vet.pdf

Espinoza, C., & Uklelja. (2016). *Managing the Millennials: Discover the Core Competencies for Managing Today's Workforce* (2nd ed.). Hoboken, NJ: John Wiley & Sons.

Feeman, M. (2016). Rewriting the Self: History, memory, narrative. New York, New York, USA: Rutledge. Retrieved April 10, 2017 from https://books.google.com/books?hl=en&lr=&id=97tmCgAAQBAJ&oi=fnd&pg=PP1&dq=describe+the+human+condition+against+our+historical+memory&ots=3yNJT9qZ4z&sig=aqtcQlActVGRltpSmG--3Uafk47E#v=onepage&q&f=false

Fleming, J. (2014, May 19). *Gallup Analysis: Millennials, Marriage and Family.* Retrieved September 30, 2017 from Gallup News: http://news.gallup.com/poll/191462/gallup-analysis-millennials-marriage-family.aspx

Flood, A. (2015). *The female millennial: a new era of talent.* PWC.

Fry, R. (2016, April 25). *Millennials overtake Baby Boomers as America's largest generation.* Retrieved June 3, 2017 from Pre Research: http://www.pewresearch.org/fact-tank/2016/04/25/millennials-overtake-baby-boomers/

Gabbard, G. O.H. (2016). The many faces of narcissism. *World Psychiatry , 15* (2), 115-116.

Gardner, H. K. (2017, May 2). *How to Capture Value from Collabora-tion, Especially If You're Skeptical About It.* Retrieved October 1, 2017 from Harvard Business Review: https://hbr.org/2017/05/ how-to-capture-value-from-collaboration-especially-if-youre-skep-tical-about-it

Generational Breakdown: Info About All of the Generations. (n.d.). Re-trieved June 3, 2017 from The Center for Generational Kinetics: http://genhq.com/faq-info-about-generations/

Generational Differences Chart. (n.d.). WMFC.org.

Gierenzer, G., & Gaissmaier, W. (2011). Heuristic Decision Making. *An-nual Review of Psychology* , 451-481.

Gilbert, J. (2011, Sept/Oct). *The Millennials: A new generation of em-ployees, a new set of engagement policies.* Retrieved June 3, 2017 from Ivey Business Journal: http://iveybusinessjournal.com/publication/ the-millennials-a-new-generation-of-employees-a-new-set-of-en-gagement-policies/

Goldsmith. M. and Carter, L. (Ed.). (2010). *Best Practices in Talent Man-agement: How.* San Francisco, CA, U.S.A.: John Wiley & Sons, Inc.

Goodheart, C. .. (2010). *A new era for collaboration.* Retrieved October 4, 2017 from American Psychological Association: https://www.apa. org/monitor/2010/04/pc.aspx

Green, A. (2015, February 2). *5 Ways Employers Discourage You From Negotiating Salary.* Retrieved May 16, 2016 from U.S. News Mon-ey: http://money.usnews.com/money/blogs/outside-voices-ca-reers/2015/02/02/5-ways-employers-discourage-you-from-negoti-ating-salary

Harris, T. (1993, May-June). The Post-Capitalist Executive: An inter-view with Peter F. Drucker. *Harvard Business Review* .

Hebert, J. (26, Jan 2017). *Why Millennials Deserve More Respect at Work.* Retrieved May 13, 2017 from Fortune: http://fortune.com/2017/01/26/millennials-2/

Hofstrand, D. (2010, February). *Peter Drucker and Innovation.* From Iowa State University Extension and Outreach: http://www.extension.iastate.edu/agdm/wholefarm/html/c5-10.html

Honigman, B. (2014, March 9). *The Unexpected Value of Business Collaboration.* Retrieved October 2, 2017 from Huffington Post: http://www.huffingtonpost.com/brian-honigman/business-collaboration_b_4548950.html

Howe, N. a. (2000). *Millenials are Rising: The Next Great Generation.* New York: Vintage.

Howe, N., & Nadler, R. (2010, Aug 25). *Managing Millennials: How to Cope With a Generation of Multitaskers.* Retrieved June 20, 2017 from eremedi.com: https://www.eremedia.com/tlnt/managing-millennials-how-to-cope-with-a-generation-of-multitaskers/

Howe, N., & Strauss, W. (1991). *Generations: The History of America's Future, 1584 to 2069.* New York: William Morrow & Company.

Howe, N., & Strauss, W. (2007, July-August). The Next 20 Years: How Customer and Workforce Attitudes Will. *Harvard Business Review* , 13.

Hudson, B. T. (1994, June). *Innovation through Acquistion.* Retrieved January 13, 2017 from The Cornell H.R.A. Quarterly: http://journals.sagepub.com/doi/pdf/10.1177/001088049403500318

Hunt, V. L. (2015, Jan). *Why diversity matters.* Retrieved June 3, 2017 from McKinsey & Company: http://www.mckinsey.com/business-functions/organization/our-insights/why-diversity-matters

Infographic - Communicating in the Modern Workplace. (n.d.). Retrieved October 1, 2017 from Queens University at Charlotte: http://online.

queens.edu/online-programs/mba/resources/infographic/commu-nicating-in-the-workplace

"Pro-business," but expecting more: *The Deloitte Millennial Survey 2017.* (2017, May 13). From Deloitte: https://www2.deloitte.com/glob-al/en/pages/about-deloitte/articles/millennial-survey-pro-busi-ness-but-expecting-more.html

Jehn, K. A. (n.d.). *To Agree or Not To Agree: The Effects of Value Con-gruence, Individual Demographic Dissimilarity and Conflict on Work-group Outcomes.* Retrieved October 4, 2017 from Semantics Scholar: https://pdfs.semanticscholar.org/efe2/61d82cd4e9a0484676a8b-7396cb5974479ea.pdf

Jenkins, R. (2017, August 7). *Why Millennials Are So Entitled (Parents Are Partly Blamed).* Retrieved August 29, 2017 from Inc.: https://www.inc.com/ryan-jenkins/this-is-why-millennials-are-entitled.html

Kaneshige, T. (2013, Oct 10). *Why Managers Need to Stop Worrying and Love Millennials.* Retrieved May 13, 2017 from CIO: http://www.cio.com/article/2381827/leadership-management/why-managers-need-to-stop-worrying-and-love-millennials.html

Kiisel, T. (2012, May 16). *Gimme, Gimme, Gimme -- Millennials in the Workplace.* Retrieved June 18, 2017 from Forbes: https://www.forbes.com/sites/tykiisel/2012/05/16/gimme-gimme-gimme-millenni-als-in-the-workplace/#738daed1bcea

Kraus, L. (2017). *2016 Disability Statistics Annual.* University of New Hampshire. Durham, NH: Institute on Disability/UCED.

Kriegel, J. (2015, May 29). *Why Generational Theory Makes No Sense.* Retrieved June 14, 2017 from Forbes.com: https://www.forbes.com/sites/oracle/2015/09/29/why-generational-theo-ry-makes-no-sense/#156566678eaa

Lee Badgett, M., & others. (2013). *The Business Impact of LGBT-Supportive Workplace Policies*. Los Angeles: The Williams Institute.

Lizardo, O. (2004). The Cognitive Origins of Bourdieu's Habitus. *Journal for the Theory of Social Behaviour 34:4 , 34* (4), 375-401.

Mankins, M. (2017, March 27). *Collaboration Overload Is a Symptom of a Deeper Organizational Problem*. Retrieved September 24, 2017 from Harvard Business Review: https://hbr.org/2017/03/collaboration-overload-is-a-symptom-of-a-deeper-organizational-problem

Mashek, D. (2016, February 22). *Collaboration: It's Not What You Think*. Retrieved October 1, 2017 from Psychology Today: https://www.psychologytoday.com/blog/relationships-intimate-and-more/201602/collaboration-its-not-what-you-think

McCord, P. (2014, Jan-Feb). *How Netflix Reinvented HR*. Retrieved June 21, 2017 from Harvard Business Review: https://hbr.org/2014/01/how-netflix-reinvented-hr

Meyer, K. (2016, Jan 3). *Millennials as Digital Natives: Myths and Realities*. Retrieved May 14, 2017 from Neilsen Norman Group: https://www.nngroup.com/articles/millennials-digital-natives/

(2011). *Millennials at work: Reshaping the Workplace*. PWC.com.

Millennials in Adulthood: Detached from Institutions, Networked with Friends. (2014, March 7). Retrieved June 3, 2017 from Pew Research Center: http://www.pewsocialtrends.org/2014/03/07/millennials-in-adulthood/

Millennials: Confident. Connected. Open to Change. (2010, Feb 24). Retrieved May 13, 2017 from Pew Rsearch Center: Millennials: Confident. Connected. Open to Change

Miller, C. C. (2014, December 2). *The Divorce is Over, but the Myth Lives On*. Retrieved October 1, 2017 from The New York Times: The Upshot: https://www.nytimes.com/2014/12/02/upshot/the-divorce-surge-is-over-but-the-myth-lives-on.html

Modaity. (n.d.). Retrieved June 12, 2017 from https://multimodalityglossary.wordpress.com/multimodality/

New Times for Multimodality? Confronting the Accountability Culture. (2012, May). *Journal of Adolescent & Adult Literacy* , 8.

Nuwer, R. (2014, April 8). *Andy Warhol Probably Never Said His Celebrated "Fifteen Minutes of Fame" Line.* Retrieved June 11, 2017 from Smithsonian Magazine: http://www.smithsonianmag.com/smart-news/andy-warhol-probably-never-said-his-celebrated-fame-line-180950456/

Onion, R. (2015, May 15). *Against generations.* Retrieved June 14, 2017 from AEON.com: https://aeon.co/essays/generational-labels-are-lazy-useless-and-just-plain-wrong

Pappas, S. (2016, Feb 8). *Why Are Millennials Narcissistic? Blame Income Inequality.* Retrieved July 20, 2017 from LiveScience.com: https://www.livescience.com/53635-why-millennials-are-narcissistic.html

Parket, K. C. (2017, April 13). *6 facts about the U.S. military and its changing demographics.* Retrieved October 1, 2017 from Pew Research C enter: https://www.pewresearch.org/fact-tank/2017/04/13/6-facts-about-the-u-s-military-and-its-changing-demographics/

Patten, E., & Fry, R. (2015). *How Millennials today compare with their grandparents 50 years ago.* Pew Research Center.

PepsiCo Earnings Preview: Snacks Could Offset Decline In Beverage Sales. (2014, February 11). Retrieved January 16, 2017 from Forbes: http://www.forbes.com/sites/greatspeculations/2014/02/11/pepsico-earnings-preview-snacks-could-offset-decline-in-beverage-sales/#7acac6e12d65

PepsiCo. (2016). *PepsiCo Reports Third Quarter 2016 Results.* PepsiCo.

Perna, M. (2016, Mar 5). *Millennials & Respect: Why It Matters So Much.* Retrieved May 16, 2017 from Linkedin: https://www.linkedin.com/pulse/millennials-respect-why-matters-so-much-mark-perna

Pisker, L. (2017, Jan 18). *Challenging Modern Society: Disabled Millennials*. Retrieved June 3, 2017 from Yout Time Magazine: http://www. youth-time.eu/articles-opinions/challenging-modern-society-disabled-millennials

Ponteriero, C. (2016, June 17). *11 institutions trusted more by millennials*. Retrieved June 12, 2017 from Property and Casuality 360°: http:// www.propertycasualty360.com/2016/06/17/11-institutions-trusted-more-by-millennials

Rebell, R. (2016, Oct 10). *RPT-COLUMN-For millennials, adulthood now defined by financial freedom*. Retrieved July 22, 2017 from Reuters. com: http://www.reuters.com/article/column-money-adulthood-repeat-column-per-idUSL1N1CG1AS?type=companyNews

Ryan, S. (2017, July 1). *New Report: Millennials' Political Behavior Will Surprise You*. Retrieved September 28, 2017 from Huffington Post: http://www.huffingtonpost.com/ryan-scott/new-report-millennials-po_b_10764426.html

Sasse, B. (2017). *The vanishing American Adult: Our Coming of Age Crisis - and How to Rebuid a Culture of Self-Reliance*. New York: St. Martin;s Press.

Stein, J. (2013, May 20). *MIllennials: The Me Me Me Generation*. Retrieved July 22, 2017 from Time.com: http://time.com/247/millennials-the-me-me-me-generation/

Suarez, J. G. (2016, Nov 24). *A baby boomer's guide to managing millennials at work*. Retrieved June 12, 2017 from Los Angeles Times: http:// www.latimes.com/business/la-fi-career-coach-boomers-millennials-20161124-story.html

Sundar, S. S. (2008). "The MAIN Model: A Heuristic Approach to Understanding Technology Effects on Credibility". (M. Flanagin, J. Metzge, & A. J., Eds.) *Digital Media* , 73-100.

Sweeney, R. (2006). Millennial Behaviors & Demographics. 1-10. Newark, NJ.

The Keys to Unlocking the Millennial Mindset. (2016, Sept. 8). Retrieved June 13, 2017 from Nielsen.com: http://www.nielsen.com/us/en/insights/news/2016/keys-to-unlocking-the-millennial-mindset.html

Tilley, P. W. (2016, June). Nietzsche's Perspectivism in Truth and Narrative. 1-13. Sidney, Australia.

Tulgan, B. (2013). Meet Generation Z: The second generation within the giant "Millennial" cohort. Retrieved June 18, 2017 from Rainmaker Thinking: http://www.rainmakerthinking.com/assets/uploads/2013/10/Gen-Z-Whitepaper.pdf

Twenge, J. (2006). Generation Me: Why Today's Young Americans are More Confident, Assertive, Entitled – and More Miserable than Ever Before. New York: Free Press.

United States. (n.d.). Retrieved June 3, 2017 from Census Reporter: https://censusreporter.org/profiles/01000US-united-states/

What is Respect to a Millennial, a Boomer, and a Gen X'er? (2016, February 16). Retrieved August 29, 2017 from U.S. Chamber of Commerce Foundation: http://institute.uschamber.com/is-respect-different-for-millennials/

When It Comes to Politics, Do Millennials Care About Anything? (n.d.). Retrieved September 22, 2017 from The Atlantic: http://www.theatlantic.com/sponsored/allstate/when-it-comes-to-politics-do-millennials-care-about-anything/255/

Williams, T. (n.d.). Racial Diversity: There's More Work to be Done in the Workplace. Retrieved jUNE 3, 2017 from The Economist: https://execed.economist.com/blog/industry-trends/racial-diversity-there%E2%80%99s-more-work-be-done-workplace

Wilson, M. a. (2008). How Generational Theory Can Improve Teaching: Strategies for Working with the "Millennials". *Curresnts in Teaching and Learnng , 1* (1), 29-44.

Zagenczyk, T. J. (2017). *The Moderating Effect of Psychological Contract Violation on the Relationship between Narcissism and Outcomes: An Application of Trait Activation Theory.* Retrieved July 22, 2017 from Frontiers in Psychology.

Chapter 9

MILLENNIALS: YOUR GREATEST OPPORTUNITY OR YOUR GREATEST THREAT

MILLENNIALS NOW REPRESENT the largest segment of our population. As one of them, I see a paradox in this. Their numbers mean power enough to govern any negotiation. But, the myths, misconceptions, and misnomers just get in the way of any sensible accommodation in the workplace.

In this book, I have provided evidence where useful to clarify the actual as opposed to the imagined, rumored, and illogical. And, I'd like to review the challenges and how businesses can manage them for mutual profit.

Numbers: The generation is calculated on many inconsistent bases. Some include Generations X and Y; some do not. Some start at one date and others at another. But, Howe and Strauss, who may be credited with starting the mess, put the start date as those born in 1982 and through the 20 years after.

With no certain way of dating the group and the U.S. Census not demarcating generations, we know those who reached young adulthood after 2000 represent big numbers. In marketing research, their every move, trend, or habit has become a closely watched metric.

Unfortunately, too many social scientists have treated the same numbers with the marketing discipline. Human behavior amounts to much more than shopping behavior; it is too varied, too spontaneous, and too beholden to too many other factors.

This has led to an unsubstantiated assumption that the generation acts as one in the workplace. It labels their behavior, controls expectations, and diminishes value. While every generation has identifying characteristics, they are typically known in retrospect. The Great Generation, for instance, was not defined by its buying habits.

Depending so much on descriptive and prescriptive analytics, critics prejudge and short-change Millennials based on the logical fallacy that what is true of an individual must be true of the whole group. Many Baby Boomers who hold power positions through talent and/or seniority struggle with such bias. At worst, their ornery resistance damages the enterprise. But, even at best, they struggle to manage what they have trouble understanding.

In addition, the Millennial population has put them into work roles that replace, push, and confront their elders. This climate of confusion and conflict, occasioned by their defining presence, is why we must deal with Millennials in the workplace. They must be paid attention—a role they enjoy.

Multimodal: Millennials bring their multimodal mindset to the workforce. They have developed as talented multi-taskers able to watch monitors intently while aggressively exploiting their eye-hand coordination to win games. They gamely listen to music, do research, and text friends at the same time—somehow not losing pace.

As children of divorce, they perform chores without question, accept assignments willingly, and want immediate recognition. Some consider this unfocused and undisciplined, but the habits are inter-disciplinary and trans-disciplinary. They juggle, blend, and weave interests, tasks, and objectives.

There is no business value in inhibiting or restricting this apparent spontaneity. The only management challenge is how much to let happen and how much to direct. Some consider this chaotic and anxious but this agility and flexibility also represents the inclination to disrupt: a value-added occasion for innovation.

Many Millennials are heuristic thinkers. As linear coders, they have absolute confidence the logic of technology will lead to solutions. It started with getting from one side of the monitor screen to the other. Angry Birds®, Super Mario Brothers®, and Minecraft™ increased the challenge. While some dug deeper into strategy dealing with variations on Dungeons and Dragons™, most waged virtual warfare in increasingly realistic scenarios.

Their gaming experience has been linear, programmed incrementally on planes where dimension is an illusion. When each move earns badges, bells, and whistles, they did not have time to ponder, meditate, or contemplate. But, the reward system leads to expectations of immediate and proportionate recognition.

It makes them relentlessly optimistic about finding answers given the time and the tools to get there. Problem-solving means project-management, and that orientation tries the patience of their predecessors.

Resulting groups and individual conflicts need prudent management that does not short-circuit this neurology. It takes the maturity of senior workers to mentor and acculturate them into holistic environments.

Creating a workplace with psychological safety, employers can channel the Millennial energy. Creating a multi-dimensional picture of the individual's career path towards the completion of the organization's vision keeps employees engaged and improves their tenure. And, listening constructively to the wisdom of their crowd will profit all parties involve.

If you find them impatient, results-oriented, and hyperactive, it's time to accept these as virtues. The virtues mark them as agile and flexible, quick to follow direction, and appreciative of mentoring. And, when you accept these values as important to your organization you can position them to reverse mentor, so everyone benefits.

Respect: Statistics report that Millennials are the best educated generation. But, that doesn't stand. Yes, more finish college and they have accumulated more hours and credentials. But, total course hours do not equal quality education. Given the opportunity, they seek to expedite learning, sometimes sacrificing depth to speed.

Like other generations, they seem older to themselves, heavily experienced by parental divorce, continuing war, economic recession, and international terrorism. Living very much in their present and believing the present contains their future, they see no relevance in history.

With universal knowledge available to them, they feel entitled to the intelligence they want. If what they want is what they find useful, they are not as smart as they think. But, if they remain the prime judge of what is useful to their ends they define what is empowering.

It follows, then, they feel no obligation to abide by familial, religious, or political traditions. They do not belong to anything they have been born into. That's not to say that they have no interest in the spiritual, polity, or other social forces, but they look for religion in churches without walls, politics without parties, and communities needing volunteers.

In fact, Millennials are present in all standard institutions except those dominated by seniority, including civil service, unions, and college faculties. They perceive themselves as independent of history, and this standalone attitude rubs others the wrong way. Because the past is irrelevant Millennials are not sentimental, and this can appear as detached and insensitive

Having always lived with computers, they underestimate their addiction and refuse to let it interfere with their perceived independence. Technology makes all things possible. Anything not discoverable through technology is irrelevant to solving problems or advancing projects.

They have turned collaboration into an institution. Their best model for collaboration is the relationship they once had with siblings who introduced them to and coached them on video games. They appreciate the give and take and pointed advice and feedback, and they appreciate advice from any source offered with that same generosity.

Millennials expect formal and informal learning to be reciprocal, challenging, engaging, and purposeful. They particularly appreciate the advice of established employees if it is offered as peer-to-peer.

Organizations that want to attract and retain such talent must present a continuing dynamic. Millennials want a sense of place where organizational purpose aligns with their knowledge, skills, and abilities. They seek institutions that have not ossified and that offer flexible life-work opportunities. And, they prefer to be an active participant in the creation of purpose-driven institutions.

Management strategies lie in creating a blended, purpose-driven climate where work produces high impact outcomes, where it serves higher core values, where an achievable career path can be drawn, and where respect is reciprocal.

Digital Natives: Born into the Age of Information, Millennials have computers in their DNA. On the positive side, this gifts them with the abilities required for future growth in a digital-economy. On the negative side, their consequent behaviors risk isolation and alienation.

It means they work forward on horizontal fields; it puts everyone on the same level without hierarchy. They share and expect sharing in return. Disappointed in social institutions, they look for stability, authenticity, and values.

Like the Boomers who work with them, they think everyone thinks as they do. They expect clarity and engagement in the work more than their elders. So, too, their idea of privacy and intellectual property differ. They expect everything known to be common property.

This sense of technology enables "the wisdom of the crowds" that rates movies, sports teams, teachers, restaurants, and much more. And, they assume their individual opinions speak for the whole. Unfortunately, that same self-certainty contributes to unwanted office chatter, cyberbullying, and unsolicited opinion.

Their digital work contributes to a perception that they work as hard or more than others. It entitles them to blur life and work. This lets them work 24/7 which may or may not align with business needs or goals. The established co-workers often see this apparent business as counterproductive.

Management's best option is to optimize Millennials' digital power, leveraging it for competitive value. At the same time, management must know how to leverage their interest and skills so that both management and Millennials benefit.

Management needs to create an environment, a branded image of a place where people want to work. The website must engage with stories of people, community sharing, and authenticated core values.

The business must structure a psychologically safe environment in which management assumes responsibility for training and developing soft and social skills. It must launch a continuing system of acculturation in which new and established workers have common tasks and goals.

Millennials may need introduction on business practices, ethics, and propriety. They must understand the importance of privacy and intellectual property. Still, management should communicate those concerns in the media and methods Millennials find engaging. So, one way to assure this connection is to bring Millennials into the conversation of priorities and method—immediately.

Narcissism: Perhaps the most prominent misconception about Millennials, the one most difficult to dispel, is the claim that they are narcissistic. The myth continues the feeling they are fundamentally unlikeable and pathologically disagreeable.

Taking a selfie does not make a narcissist. Ambitious, self-confident, outspoken, and optimistic, they bring a value-added energy. They do differ from the homogenize Baby Boomer generation. They are not highly structured or stratified. Millennials are active and articulate, and they can be pesky asking, "Why?"

Self-aware and self-conscious, they resent implications that they are egotists, selfish, and self-centered. Heads-up managers, understand Millennials are not narcissistic as a class or more than their elders.

Closer to the evidence is the understanding that they may lag their chronological age in terms of social skills and emotional intelligence. That helps you handle their energy and charism, but it also calls for a deep and broad realignment of management practices.

Institutions: It is true that Millennials are not your parents' generation. On one hand, Millennials belong to a most diverse and democratized generation. On the other hand, some of them participate in this most segmented and divisive culture. The generation staffs Doctors Without Borders, but they also drive alt-right and alt-left politics.

Standard institutions have failed Millennials. Born into a culture of divorce, prolonged war, banking collapse, and religious scandals, they still appreciate the organizational function of institution. But, they want to own their own.

Their inclination to self-express does not mean disrespect or defiance. It seeks attention and acknowledgement, and it questions why feedback is rejected or ignored. However, they will defer to people and decisions they respect.

They will also support institutions that pursue clear purpose, make collaboration the central means to achievement, and promote egalitarianism. Optimistic about the future as they are, they reject and resist institutions that stand in the way of their collective power.

Different forces have shaped their thinking. They measure things differently than their predecessors. They are less inclined to stick with things until they get better, and they expect performance—not consistency—from institutions.

Management must realize Millennials are not a homogenous class. The best of them are flexible, adaptive, and resilient. They want to be heard and appreciated; that means accepting and integrating their feedback.

They understand collaboration better than their elders. They bring collegiality to teamwork making it more valuable than committee work. And, in a truly collaborative culture, hierarchical titles mean nothing. They feel they have a right to the resources they need and seek authenticity in leadership that frames purpose.

Businesses with transparent commitment to purpose build institutions that inspire the loyalty and commitment of Millennial employees. They must want to work with your business to achieve something of value.

Collaboration: When a business values collaborative tactics, it sustains a psychologically safe environment. Collaboration is an ethos Millennials grew into and carry with them. They almost do not understand another way.

They understand collaboration to be a group problem-solving process. It requires active participation in a sharing environment where creative, functional, and innovative contributions deserve feedback and integration.

This joint work assumes trust and consensus building on the part of members working in coalitions, alliances, and partnerships. It encourages disagreement and dialog that develop synergies and solutions. But, this psychology requires management actively committed to and interested in the process and outcomes. They must make the exercise more important and effective than an exercise in connectivity.

Leadership charged with the architecture for collaboration will model peer-to-peer communication. Such managers must lead communication that regularly revisits purpose, plan, and process discussing accountability, individual and group roles, and the values of feedback and diverse views.

Successful mangers allow members to select their leaders and assign accountabilities to increase their buy-in. They measure and reward individual contributions. Rewards must recognize collaborative contributions, not individual work or efforts, the quality not the quantity of collaborative performance.

Millennials give priority to the wisdom of the crowd—more than they know. While this may run counter to their elders' emphasis on individuality and self-reliance, it does produce undeniable benefits.

Innovation thrives on collaboration. It is the accepted way of life in a digital age. It makes invaluable the diversity that enables and fuels it.

In a world of global competition, all work must be co-created. And, only those businesses encouraging and facilitating collaboration will attract and retain Millennials.

MAKING PEACE WITH MILLENNIALS

The sheer size of the Millennial workforce gives them an edge in managing the work of the future. To make your business succeed, it must align with that future. Success depends on your ability to optimize what Millennials bring to the table.

However, you cannot manage the generation if you are bound by the rampant myths and misconceptions about the group. Pejorative language, poor evidence, and cultural bias have bound their usefulness.

Every accusation ignores strengths and energies that can revolutionize an organization. It takes understanding, patience, and willingness on the part of senior leadership to welcome Millennials into a sustaining and innovative process.

Finally, leadership must make its commitment dynamic, flexible, and agile. Otherwise, it is left to merely manage its tried, true, and self-defeating status.

CPSIA information can be obtained
at www.ICGtesting.com
Printed in the USA
LVHW01s0244020318
568402LV00003B/3/P